What People Are Saying About *Business Climate Shifts*

"Today's business world is rife with upheaval and turbulence. In this environment, companies must learn to manage change as never before. This book is essential reading if you want to master the intricacies of reengineering or corporate transformation in your organization and energize your employees as part of that process."
—**Lord Colin Marshall**, Chairman, British Airways

"Change, of course, is the one certainty in business today. Globalization, new technologies, emerging markets, and the need for speed in getting new products *to* market are all driving companies to excel as never before. This book details how any company—in any industry—can effectively transform its operations, align people, and improve employee productivity and bottom-line profitability as a result."
—**Lee Griffin**, CEO, Bank One of Louisiana

"This book provides fascinating glimpses into some of the most significant and successful change efforts of recent years. I think this is a 'must read' for any senior business leader managing change."
—**Fred Poses**, President, AlliedSignal

"Engaging, thoughtful, and practical, this book provides insights and ideas that any CEO will find useful in managing corporate transformation initiatives. Well worth reading!"
—**Robert Bauman**, former CEO, SmithKline Beecham

"Managing successful organizational change is a complex, multi-dimensional process. This book provides a wonderful roadmap for helping you harness the 'engines' of organizational transformation in your *own* company. I highly recommend!"

—**Sir Richard Evans**, Chairman, British Aerospace

"In my personal dealings with Bill Trahant I have been continually impressed by his ability to relate intellectual models and concepts to the practicalities of day-to-day operations and the effect on individuals. He is one of those remarkable people who truly understands the dilemmas of leadership."

—**Errol Marshall**, Chairman, Shell South Africa (PTY) Ltd.

"Authors Trahant and Burke have taken a novel approach in this book. They sat down with a wide variety of their clients and got them to describe, in their own words, what made them successful in managing business change. The result is some great storytelling, some great journalism, and a mother lode of insights that you can use to manage transformation or reengineering efforts in your *own* company!"

—**Mac McDonald**, Director, Leadership & Performance Operation, Shell International B.V.

"Developing leaders for global responsibilities requires an in-depth understanding of those who have become role models for organizational change. In *Business Climate Shifts*, the authors have captured the essence of leadership for the 21st century. This is an important guide for anyone concerned with executive education."

—**Stephen H. Rhinesmith**, Former Chairman, American Society for Training and Development

"The voices of these successful champions of change speak loud and clear: resistance to change is futile. Recognize it. Get ahead of it. Turn it into competitive advantage. Then start all over again. They tell how it's done."
—**John Dimsdale**, Washington Bureau Chief, "Marketplace", Public Radio International

"Giant multinationals need to transform themselves to survive. This is not a book about the theory of how management might do this. These are real life stories of how it has been done. Other corporations, struggling with their own reforms, should listen and learn from these experiences."
   —**Hamish McRae**, Associate Editor, *The Independent*, London

"An expertly crafted analysis of the myriad aspects of organizational change, *Business Climate Shifts* offers an enlightening and reader-friendly guide to the innovative approaches taken by today's transformational leaders."
   —**Mary Ann C. Fusco**, Editor, *National Productivity Review*

"A fascinating examination of how different companies in different industries have successfully managed change. The interviews are absorbing and filled with important learnings about change that CEO's and change agents can use in virtually *any* organization!"
—**Robert S. Morgan**, President, Council of Growing Companies

Business Climate Shifts

Profiles of Change Makers

W. Warner Burke and William Trahant
with Richard Koonce

BUTTERWORTH
HEINEMANN

BOSTON OXFORD AUCKLAND JOHANNESBURG MELBOURNE NEW DELHI

**BUTTERWORTH
HEINEMANN**

A member of the Reed Elsevier group
Copyright © 2000 by PricewaterhouseCoopers

Recognizing the importance of preserving what has been written, Butterworth–Heinemann prints its books on acid-free paper whenever possible.

 Butterworth–Heinemann supports the efforts of American Forests and the Global ReLeaf program in its campaign for the betterment of trees, forests, and our environment.

Library of Congress Cataloging-in-Publication Data

Burke, Warner.
 Business climate shifts : profiles of change makers / Warner
Burke, William Trahant with Richard Koonce.
  p. cm.
 Includes bibliographical references and index.
 ISBN 0-7506-7186-6 (hardcover : alk. paper)
 1. Chief executive officers–Case studies. 2. Management—Case
studies. 3. Organizational change. 4. Industrial management.
5. Decision making. I. Trahant, William. II. Koonce, Richard.
III. Title.
HD38.2.B865 1999
658.4′063—dc21   99-37788
                                                             CIP

British Library Cataloguing-in-Publication Data
A catalogue record for this book is available from the British Library.

The publisher offers special discounts on bulk orders of this book.
For information, please contact:

Manager of Special Sales
Butterworth–Heinemann
225 Wildwood Avenue
Woburn, MA 01801–2041
Tel: 781-904-2500
Fax: 781-904-2620

For information on all Butterworth–Heinemann publications available, contact our World Wide Web home page at: http://www.bh.com

SixSigma™ is a registered trademark of Motorola.
Book cover design inspired by Diana Galligan.

10 9 8 7 6 5 4 3 2 1

Printed in the United States of America

CONTENTS

FOREWORD

We're living through a time of tremendous sea changes in business. Globalization, the disruptive influence of new technologies, the emergence of e-business, and growing electronic connectivity among far-flung financial markets are all accelerating the pace of commerce throughout the world today—in virtually every industry.

Add deregulation, political instability, emerging new economies in the Pacific Rim, and an exploding number of new scientific discoveries (many of which lead quickly to new products and commercial applications), and you have a recipe not only for market turbulence, but also for what this book's authors describe as "disruptive phase shifts" in how business is conducted.

In *Business Climate Shifts: Profiles of Change Makers*, Bill Trahant of PricewaterhouseCoopers Consulting and W. Warner Burke of Teachers College, Columbia University explain that "phase shifts"—critical discontinuities that occur in the life of a business as the result of accelerated deployment of new technologies or the rapid emergence of new business competitors—can spell the death knell for companies. This, if they fail to adapt rapidly to a changing business climate.

So, how can a company survive and thrive in today's business climate, given that the nature of change *itself* keeps changing?

Many companies don't. Some grow complacent, certain that their market dominance is assured. Others fall out of step with changing customer tastes, or fail to find and exploit new markets (e.g., overseas or online). Others fail for lack of leadership resolve or imagination, or because the imperative of "continuous transformation" never takes root as a core business value, essential to the long-term health and profitability of the company.

By contrast, today's smartest and most resilient companies (many of which the authors profile in their book) are those that don't take anything for granted. They are "environmentally vigilant." They become masters of "organizational retransformation," periodically restructuring or realigning themselves in response to changing market or business conditions. Most important, their leaders create powerful "climates of internal alignment" to support achievement of their business or change goals.

In *Business Climate Shifts: Profiles of Change Makers*, you'll meet a select group of these "change makers"—some of the most successful transformational leaders of our day—and learn first-hand their secrets for leading highly successful business transformation efforts. For instance, you'll hear Colin Marshall describe how he turned British Airways from a tired, demoralized air carrier into one of the world's most successful and profitable airlines. You'll learn first-hand from Bob Bauman how he successfully orchestrated a "merger of equals" between U.S.-based SmithKline Beckman and British-based Beecham. You'll hear Errol Marshall outline how he's using the "emotional" power of the "Shell brand" to unite and galvanize employees of Shell South Africa in order to help that company succeed in a country that's moving swiftly from Third World nation to a world-class economy. And you'll learn how U.S. Postmaster General Bill Henderson has turned the U.S. Postal Service into a highly profitable enterprise, and why he thinks the emergence of the Internet will ultimately provide a boom in business for America's postal service.

The authors provide profiles of these and many other highly successful transformational leaders in this powerful book. But it contains more than just probing profiles of highly successful "change leaders." You'll also find powerful tools and techniques to manage successful transformation in your *own* company or organization.

In *Business Climate Shifts: Profiles of Change Makers* the authors have clearly identified two of the most important factors in organizational resilience: alignment and agility. In today's business world the former without the latter doesn't work because that represents the old command/control model of organizations. And agility without alignment won't work because that can make an organization's actions error-prone and chaotic.

Business Climate Shifts will help you develop the competencies you need to be an effective change maker in your *own* organization while steering your company to new growth, prosperity, and markets in the next millennium. You'll learn about the change challenges facing business executives in a variety of industries. At the same time, you'll derive wisdom that you can use to transform your own organization into a nimbler, more "change-capable" enterprise.

Warren Bennis
Distinguished Professor of Business
University of Southern California

PREFACE

In today's rapidly changing business world, where the nature of change *itself* is continuously changing, it's sometimes difficult to "codify" the components of effective change leadership. So, we tend to be inspired by example. GE's Jack Welch and AlliedSignal's Larry Bossidy are two examples that have captured the popular business imagination and that tend to be the wellspring of many executives' creative inspiration about change leadership.

Yet, as informative as these examples are, other highly successful transformational leaders are out there today—in a variety of fields and industries—whose own track records of success with change leadership provide a rich tapestry of experience from which executives can draw important lessons and insights, and which in many cases may be more relevant to their own change challenges.

This book contains portraits of these "change makers." And regardless of whether you work in energy or aerospace, in pharmaceuticals or in manufacturing, in the private sector or the public arena, it's our hope that by reading about the experiences of these change leaders you'll distill important learnings and ideas that you can apply to the change challenges you face in your *own* organization.

In our view, there's no simple "shake-and-bake" recipe or rule by which to lead successful change efforts. For the craft of change leadership is as much a human art as it is a management science. It requires imagination and emotional involvement on a leader's part as much as it does discipline and focus, and it relies as much on a leader's personal openness to new learning—as a change initiative proceeds—as it does on enthusiastic and committed employees.

Having said that, this book is less a management or methodology text than it is a series of "stories" about leaders who have led highly successful and memorable change efforts. To complete this book, we interviewed some of our most interesting and challenging clients, and have presented those interviews here as "conversations" on which we invite you to listen in. Presenting the case studies this way, we feel, provides dimensionality to each of these change leaders not only as executives but also as *people*. In each instance, you'll learn about the challenges and obstacles they faced, and hear each individual describe, in his or her own words, what makes for successful leadership of organizational change.

In many cases, as you'll see, the individual change challenges they face are quite different; yet common themes run throughout all the case studies—the theme of "leader as learner" being one, the importance of communicating the urgency of change to employees being another, the importance of creating a "climate of internal alignment" to support change initiatives being still another. Each chapter provides some important industry context for the challenges that individual executives faced and a "Chapter Conclusions" section in which the key learnings from that chapter are summarized for your convenience. The book concludes with an Epilogue in which we outline what we view as some of the significant business "climate shifts" that executives and managers will face in the future, and in which we describe the skills and traits that will make for the successful change makers of tomorrow.

We hope you enjoy this book and find it a useful guide as you navigate the roiling waters of change in your own industry and organization.

The Authors

ACKNOWLEDGEMENTS

Writing a book is nothing if not a group effort. Many people were involved in helping to make this book a reality, and we want to thank all those who helped in its conception and development.

First of all, we want to thank our clients, all of whom shared their wisdom and gave graciously of their time for interviews. Without you, this book wouldn't have been possible. We particularly want to thank Lee Griffin and Betty Hanks of Bank One of Louisiana; at Royal Dutch Shell, Mac McDonald, Errol Marshall, Roz Douglas, Sharron Brown, and Bruno Cointepas; at BTR, Bob Bauman and Val Delany; Colin Marshall of British Airways; Sandy Gardiner of Gardiner Consulting; at British Aerospace, Dick Evans and Anne McCarthy; at the United States Postal Service, Bill Henderson, Frank Brennan, and Sally Jozwiak; at AlliedSignal, Fred Poses, Donnee Ramelli, Millie Asencio, Joelle Strona, and Jonathan Grundt; at the FAA, Jane Garvey, Ray Long, Dennis Hupp, Dana Lakeman, and Deborah Robinson; and at Global Sourcing Services, Roger Goldman.

At PricewaterhouseCoopers we want to give special thanks to Grady Means, Karen Vander Linde, Wood Parker, Steve Yearout, Dick Smith, Ian Littman, Wayne Wilhelm, Pam Weber, Susan Barborek, Shirley Cauffman, Rita Thomas, Jim Niemes, Jerry Blakeslee,

Kay McGrath, Phil Spencer, Peter Sobich, Marie Muscella, Maryline Damour, Ana Cardenas, Chris White, Doug Myers, Natalia Jefferson, Nicola Adamson, Doug Seybert, and Denise Clark.

At Burke Associates, special thanks to Mary Zippo; and at Teacher's College Columbia University, to Janis Owen.

To our friends at USAA (Julio Alfaro), Mercedes-Benz USA (Bill Hurley and Mark Juran), and Sun MicroSystems (MaryAnn Munroe and Judy Turkevich), we thank you all for your contributions to Chapter 10.

To our agent, Doris Michaels, whose enthusiasm for this project never waned, and who helped this book find a home with Butterworth–Heinemann. To our friends and editors at BH, Rita Lombard, Karen Speerstra, Tina Adoniou, Michael Abenante, Stephen Jadick, Katherine Greig, Cate Rickard Barr, and Pam Boiros, who believed in this project and helped make this book a reality. To all of you, we offer our thanks.

To our colleague at *Management Review*, Barbara Etorre, and to our friends and editors at *Training & Development* magazine, Pat Galagan and Haidee Allerton. We thank you for your professional friendship, wonderful editorial skills, and warm support of this project.

To Jim Veizis, Dino Veizis, and Alex Veizis at Video-on-Location, who helped us in capturing the video interviews that served as the basis for many of this book's chapters as well as the foundation for the PricewaterhouseCoopers Video Library. You guys did a great job. To Mary Jettner and John and Diana Galligan, for your help in reviewing manuscript drafts and in assisting with much of the behind-the-scenes administrative duties and paperwork, your help is greatly appreciated, as well.

We want to thank our wives, Bobbi Burke and Nedra Trahant, whose emotional support and words of encouragement were critical to both of us as we moved forward to develop this book's major themes. Finally, to our collaborator Richard Koonce, who gave voice to our beliefs and convictions about change management in this book. You have helped us shape this book into what we believe will be an important contribution to today's thought leadership and professional dialogue about business transformation and organizational renewal.

Our goal in writing this book has been not only to provide you with a roadmap for managing successful change, but also to showcase some of the most interesting and challenging clients that each of us has had the privilege of working with over the years. We are certain that we have learned more from them than they have from us, yet they have honored us by having us serve as their guides and companions on their change journeys.

—W. Warner Burke and William Trahant

"Opportunity comes with change. Big opportunities happen when everything is in flux. Everything is in flux now. All around us there is dislocation, stress, and the breakup of established orders. Obviously this presents a threat. Yet, for the nimble and the fearless, it presents unparalleled opportunity."

—Gerald Ross and Michael Kay, *Toppling the Pyramids*

"To compete, companies must burn themselves down every few years and rebuild their strategies, roles, and practices."

—Roger Martin

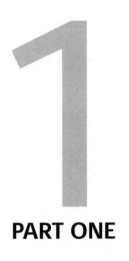

PART ONE

Change Isn't What It Used to Be

1 Phase *Shifts:* Managing Chaos and Convergence In Today's Business Environment

"We are living through a transformation that will rearrange the politics and economics of the next century. There will be no national products or technologies, no national corporations, no national industries. There will no longer be national economies, at least as we have come to understand that concept. All that will remain rooted within national borders are the people who comprise a nation. 'American' corporations and 'American' industries are ceasing to exist in any form that can meaningfully be distinguished from the rest of the global economy."

—Robert Reich, *The Work of Nations*

If you're like most people in business today—spending at least some of your waking hours each day at a computer or in cyber-space—you're familiar with Moore's Law. It's the idea, advanced by Intel Co-Founder Gordon Moore, that the power of the microchip will continue to double every 18 months, bringing with it a whole host of benefits while exponentially increasing the power of computers with each new generation of technology that is introduced into the marketplace.

Under this scenario, one can argue that Intel benefits by having to satisfy a virtually nonstop demand for chips with greater and greater memory capacities. But at the same time, all the rest of us benefit as well, as enhanced computer memory gives even palm-sized computers the capacity to do things that computers on the space shuttle couldn't do five years ago.

The notion of a "Moore's Law" is overwhelmingly convincing and seductive. We want to believe in its "logic," because we stand to benefit as much as any Intel stockholder. In coining the notion of Moore's Law, Intel executives not only managed to frame consumer expectations of what computers should be able to do with each new passing day (thus assuring themselves of a never-ending demand for their chips), but they also created a paradigm of expectations—in the minds of their customers, retail consumers of electronics products, and virtually everyone else—about what technology of *any kind* should be able to do for us.

A Metaphor for Transformational Change

We submit that Moore's Law serves yet another function today, as well. It is a metaphor for the order-of-magnitude changes taking place in business and commerce. Change is no longer linear or incremental; rather, it is rapid, discontinuous, and exponential—both in nature and in impact. Witness the "multiplier effects" and quantum leaps in how business is conducted, as technology reduces international capital transfers to computer keystrokes, as it connects markets (both mature and emerging) in instantaneous, never-before-imagined ways, and as it reduces earlier barriers to commerce (like time and distance) to meaningless anachronisms and creates new economic opportunities (and, often, new companies and industries) virtually overnight.

But it isn't just technology that is accelerating change today. Other forces—turbulence in emerging economies, business consolidation in mature industries, political instability in Russia and China, and even unanticipated scientific discoveries (in cloning, nano-technologies, drugs, and gene therapy for example)—are generating unexpected business opportunities as well as unprecedented business volatility.

The confluence of *all* these forces as marketplace dynamics has radically redrawn the business landscape in recent years. Today, the seesawing nature of emerging economies in the Pacific Rim causes wild gyrations on Wall Street on an almost daily basis. Meanwhile, hardly a day goes by without new technological breakthroughs being announced or new scientific discoveries being made with wide-ranging consequences and significant business implications.

"There was once a rule of thumb that the process of turning laboratory breakthroughs into profitable products occurs over life spans of 10 to 15 years or longer. The thinking today is that this process often occurs over lunch," says Dr. Neal Lane, Director of the National Science Foundation, who addressed a group of industrialists and information technologists in the summer of 1998. "Yesterday's experiments are today's economic engine. From penicillin to the laser, history is replete with examples of unexpected economic and societal benefits emerging from advances in fundamental science and engineering."[1]

Chaos and Convergence

All of this suggests that we are living in a time of *chaos* and *convergence*. There is *chaos* in the marketplace as companies seek strategic partnerships or restructure themselves in response to shifting capital flows, changing customer demands, and the need to find new markets for products in an age of overcapacity. In Europe, for example, in the wake of the end of the Cold War, a fragmented defense industry is trying to reconstitute itself in ways that will make it competitive in a new worldwide marketplace for armaments and defensive weapon systems. (To that end, British Aerospace, Daimler-Benz Aerospace, and Aerospatiale are battling to become a single integrated company so that they have the global reach and marketing muscle to take on the likes of Lockheed Martin and Boeing.)

Elsewhere, one sees *convergence,* as the boundaries between previously discrete industries become porous. A good illustration of this is the continual blurring and morphing of the phone, cable TV, wireless communications, software, and entertainment industries into a new corporate polyglot called "multimedia."

Another example is the growing (but still largely unacknowledged) convergence of the high-tech and biotech industries. At a world conclave of chief information officers and information technology (IT) professionals at George Mason University in 1998, Dr. Howard Frank, Dean of the University of Maryland's College of Business and Management, predicted that within a few short years we will be using "cellular" computers—composed of human cells instead of silicon—to help diagnose disease and to identify toxic materials and gases.[2] The merging of the high-tech and biotechnology fields, experts say, will bring the introduction of a vast array of new biotechnology products with potential applications in health care, pharmaceutical research, biomedical manufacturing, and many other fields.

Yes, we're living in a time of rapid and, at times, disorienting change. Occasionally, we must all play catch-up. As William Greider points out in his book *One World, Ready or Not: The Manic Logic of Global Capitalism* the essence of today's "industrial revolution, like others before it, is that commerce and finance have leapt inventively beyond the existing order and existing consciousness of peoples and societies. The global system of trade and production is fast constructing a new functional reality for most everyone's life, a new order based upon its own dynamics and not confined by the traditional social understandings. People may wish to turn away from that fact, but there is essentially no place to hide, not if one lives in any of the industrialized nations."[3]

Dealing with Phase Shifts

Change is so rapid in the business environment today that we speak of a concept we call "phase shifts" to describe just how quickly change can come to pass. Phase shifts refer to the fact that whether one is speaking of technology (e.g., the emergence of the

Internet), or unexpected scientific discoveries (e.g., cloning), or political instability in emerging markets (e.g., Russia, China, South Africa), changes can be so rapid at times as to rewrite the rules of business and commerce virtually overnight.

Certainly, this is what Andy Grove, former CEO of Intel, was talking about when he wrote about the emergence of the Internet as representing a "strategic inflection point" in the life of business. The Internet, says Grove, was already rewriting the rules of business before its full influence began to be appreciated.

It's also what Don Tapscott, author of *The Digital Economy*, was talking about when he described the multiple influences that are pressuring companies today to perform as never before. Today's "new economy," writes Tapscott, "is creating a tyranny of conflicting drivers, causing every company to rethink its mission. [A] hundred factors are pressuring the cost structure of large companies. Time to reach market is critical when products have a competitive life span of one year, one month, one week, or one afternoon, as in the case of some products in financial services. Innovation, rather than access to resources, plant, and capital, is what counts most. Customers have changed, expecting that companies must provide best quality, green products, fast, at lowest price, with best service, and ensuring social responsibility . . ."[4] For all these reasons, being able to see the future has never been more important to the success and long-term viability of companies than it is today.

It's Tough to Be a Futurist

As anyone who has ever tried to be a futurist has found, predicting the future (much less planning for it) is a difficult exercise. Many marketplace variables (e.g., poor infrastructure in emerging countries) can take years to have a detrimental effect on companies investing in emerging markets. Moreover, many technological inventions that later spawn revolutions in how business is conducted (e.g., the invention of the PC) have no readily discrete (and thus easily discernible) "event horizon" to them. Only in retrospect do we see their significance.

Even so prescient a social and business observer as Alvin Toffler, in his 1970s classic *Future Shock*, failed to anticipate the development of personal computers or the emergence of the Internet.

Today, of course, none of us can imagine being without such tools, be it to transact business or to handle even the most routine personal tasks.

Today's executives are, in many cases, unprepared to deal with the discontinuous changes taking place in the business environment. In many cases, they're operating with rulebooks written in a slower and gentler business time, when linear thinking and traditional business models more than sufficed to explain the dynamics of markets or to make routine business forecasts.

What's the solution? In our minds, it begins with you, the reader, looking *in new ways* at the external environment in which your company operates.

Today's global business environment is in reality an economic and commercial "ecosystem." Change in this system occurs as the result of different forces or "climatic elements" being in constant motion and, therefore, in constantly shifting relationship with one another. The results can affect the health and activity of markets and the profitability and competitiveness of industries and companies.

Business Climate Modeling

For that reason, we use a concept we call "business climate modeling" to analyze key variables in this business environment. For example, we think it critical that companies have a firm understanding of globalization and of the accelerating pace of scientific discoveries and technological breakthroughs that can potentially alter the marketplace balance-of-power among them and their competitors. We think it essential that firms fully appreciate the changing political and regulatory environments in which they operate and that they know how to leverage both people and technology to secure sustained profitability and long-term market viability. And we think it critical that businesspeople understand the changing nature of change *itself.*

Today's business trends "are creating a hypercompetitive international business environment that bears little resemblance to the one that existed five years ago—or that awaits us two years hence," notes Matthew Kiernan, Chairman of Innovest, a global business strategy consulting firm. "It is a world in which competition has become so ferocious, multifaceted, and unpredictable that no competitive advantage can possibly endure, but must be constantly re-created."[5]

The underlying principles of "business climate modeling" include the following:

1. *In today's business environment, a company must be willing to accept chaos or at least "bounded instability" in its industry, the global economy, and its own marketplace as part of the reality of doing business.* Today's tumult in telecommunications, in Internet commerce, and in online services exemplifies the revolutionary change sweeping across today's business landscape. Are you ready for it? Nowadays, there's no such thing as "safely harbored market share" anymore. Instead, you must be ready to deal with the rising curves of competition, technological innovation, and capital required to keep up with both.

2. *Today's global economy is in a constant state of growth and expansion characterized by both incremental change and longer-term systemic transformation.* Thus the nature of industries and markets will continue to evolve, having a significant impact on the organizational structure of companies. "Global organizations today find that, to be successful, they must stress cross-functional process more than hierarchical structure," writes Stephen Rhinesmith in his book *A Manager's Guide to Globalization.* "As a result, managers are learning to look at core competencies, value-chain management, total quality management [e.g., Six Sigma™], and many other processes that are geared to marshaling the resources of the total organization to achieve business objectives."[6]

3. *Everything today is connected and interdependent: capital, customers, companies, countries, and markets.* Therefore, you must take a "climatic perspective" to understanding the forces at work in today's business environment. As consultant and futurist, Kiernan observes: "The explosion and convergence of computing, communications, and financial technologies have created a world of instantaneous interdependence. Debt, equity, and currency markets have all become so profoundly globalized and interconnected that

when the Mexican peso catches a cold, the American dollar, Swedish kroner, and Italian lira immediately begin sneezing loudly as well."[7]

4. *In the long run, linear thinking will kill you.* As we just noted, today's business environment is a complex web of interrelated variables, acting both individually and in concert with one another. Therefore, trying to project the future, in a straight-line way, is not only not possible, but it could also prove lethal for your company.

5. *Forget hierarchies. Focus on creating an organization that's built for speed and for customers.* To survive and thrive in tomorrow's business climate, companies in every industry will need to reduce cycle times, streamline research and development processes, and forge much closer ties to their customers if they want to secure market share. Several of the companies we profile later in this book (e.g., British Aerospace, British Airways, and AlliedSignal) have learned how to do this very well.

6. *Organizations must develop "organizational intelligence" about the constantly shifting business environments in which they operate.* Knowledge and how you leverage it inside an organization is the key to sustained competitive advantage today. The most successful organizations (many of which we profile in this book) have learned how to share information efficiently, revise "best practices" on a rapid and continuous basis, build intimate relationships with customers, and create strong links between employee performance and organizational performance. This goes for companies such as drug-maker SmithKline Beecham as well as for public sector agencies such as the United States Postal Service.

7. *Business is shifting from being about "transactions" to being about "value-added" interactions with customers.* Companies that are today's customer service "superstars" (e.g., USAA, Mercedes-Benz, and Sun MicroSystems, whom we profile in Chapter 10) are those that have learned to use even routine contacts with customers to cement closer relationships with those customers. Finally:

8. *In a world where most products and services ultimately become commodities, customer care becomes the only true and lasting differentiator.*

Creating a Change-Capable Organization

Companies that subscribe to the above "rules of engagement" in business today are what we refer to as "change capable." They have both the business savvy and organizational resources to continuously adapt themselves in response to changing business and marketplace conditions. But they do even more:

Change-capable organizations:

- Use circumstances of marketplace turbulence to enhance organizational learning, improve best practices, and leverage knowledge of customers and competitors
- Let "service to customers" drive their organizational structure
- Leverage the traits of both charismatic and instrumental leadership to successfully drive change initiatives
- Ensure that teamwork takes root as a core work value
- Use multiple metrics to monitor and gauge success with change
- Successfully manage both the "hard" (metrics and goals) and "soft" (people and performance) aspects of change projects
- Ensure there is synergy around people, systems, and technology
- Make sure employees understand what change means for them
- Create explicit two-way "employment contracts" with employees to ensure they have the motivated work forces they need to succeed

"What If" Scenarios

In coming chapters of *Business Climate Shifts*, you'll learn more about many of today's most "change-capable" organizations. You'll learn how they transformed themselves in many cases from underperformers into performance and earnings superstars—by taking stock of changes in the external business environment and adapting themselves accordingly.

How can *your* company do the same? It's tempting, of course, to try and predict the future as accurately as one can; however, it's more important to construct alternative scenarios of the future for which your company can then prepare.

The value of scenario planning in business cannot be overstated today, especially as the business environment grows increasingly complex and interdependent. That's because scenario planning deals not just with facts but also with perceptions. It invites the imagination and intuition to inform companies' decision-making processes and, in so doing, creates breakthrough awareness of potential events that are usually outside one's everyday frame of reference. "If the planners of Three Mile Island had written a story about how things could go wrong instead of a numeric analysis of possible fault sequences, they would have been prepared for the surprise they actually encountered when their complex machine went astray," writes Peter Schwartz in *The Art of the Long View.*[8]

In that spirit, consider these hypothetical business scenarios, any of which could come to pass in the not-too-distant future:

Scenario #1: Cuba as the Hong Kong of the Western Hemisphere

Imagine what would happen if the United States suddenly dropped its 35-year-old trade embargo against Cuba and, if at the same time, there was a breakthrough agreement between Havana and Washington that led to the United States and Cuba becoming fast friends and business partners. Such a possibility was floated more than a few times in the weeks and months following the Pope's January 1998 visit to Cuba.

How would such developments affect the flow of international business between North and South America? Would Cuba emerge as a kind of Hong Kong of the Western hemisphere, acting not only as a new virgin market for U.S. products and services, but also as a commercial "portal," supporting expanded levels of trade between the United States and its hemispheric neighbors to the South? With many business analysts already speculating about the nature of a post-Castro Cuba, this kind of scenario may be closer to coming true than we think.

What would be the bottom-line impact of this scenario for your company? Your industry? The ramifications would probably be significant if you work in the tourism industry, the soft drink or import-export industry, in agriculture, or in consumer electronics.

Scenario #2: Will Iran Become Another China?

Now consider what would happen if the United States and Iran began to have normal cultural and business relations again. Some observers have predicted that this will soon happen, as that country's fundamentalist Islamic leaders give way to political realists more bent on trade and commercial interaction with the West.

Would this help build bridges of better understanding to the peoples of the Middle East and, in turn, open their economies up for international investment by American firms once again? And what are the chances that this could affect *your* company's global business operations in some way? Probably quite high. As more and more companies go global, you can be sure that everybody from credit card companies and business couriers to Pepsi, Benetton, and McDonald's will be ponying up for closer ties with a consumer marketplace that's been largely cut off from the rest of the world for the last 20 years.

As we write these words, a U.S. wrestling team has recently visited Iran to participate in an international sports event there, the first such visit by a U.S. athletic team to that country in nearly 20 years. You may recall that it was just 30 years ago during the Nixon administration that another sports team, a ping-pong team, acted as the advance squad for the opening up of China to international business and cultural exchanges.

Scenario #3: Is There a Future for "Pharming"?

Now consider what's likely to happen in the next five years in the drug, chemical, and biotech industries as the cloning technology first demonstrated with "Dolly" the sheep in 1997 is refined and finds its way into different business and consumer applications in industries like pharmaceuticals and biometrics.

In January 1997, just a little less than a year after the successful cloning of Dolly was announced, *The New York Times*
reported the cloning of "George" and "Charlie," two geneti-
cally engineered Holsteins, using a refinement of the
"Dolly" technology that is likely to have broad and lucra-
tive medical benefits.

At the time, cloning experts believed that the two calves
would become the foundation for a whole new industry
known as "pharming." Pharming involves the creation of
genetically-altered animals that act as living drug factories,
producing valuable pharmaceutical components in their
milk, or as living organ factories, providing organs that can
be engineered to resist rejection by the human immune
system. "I look at this as being a major step toward the
commercialization of the technology," noted Dr. James
Robl of Advanced Cell Technology, a biotech start-up in
Worcester, Massachusetts, whose firm undertook the
experiment.[9]

Today, a firm named PPL Therapeutics, the U.S. offshoot of
the Scottish company whose scientists cloned Dolly, has
put down roots in Blacksburg, Virginia. "While ethicists
have been debating human cloning, while legislators have
been considering bans, and while pastors have been inveigh-
ing against tampering with God's creation," *The Washington Post* reports, "PPL scientists have been quietly plugging
away in barns and pastures, trying to sidestep the contro-
versy. They see cloning as a quick, efficient way to produce
animals with special genetic traits that can solve health
problems, and as a potential profitable business."[10]

Climate Shifts Can Occur Easily and Unexpectedly

Events like those we've just described can, when they occur (or
reach critical mass), greatly impact the business climate—not just
for one company, but for an entire industry and even the world
economy. In other cases, they can fundamentally alter the marketplace "balance-of-power" among competitors, turn fledgling business start-ups into powerhouse business players, or signal the death

knell for one industry and the rise of others. Remember when computer giant Dell Computer was just a struggling start-up?

In essence, they can create *discontinuities* in the development of both societies and systems of business and commerce, the full effects of which can be tough to anticipate. Remember what happened to buggy-whip manufacturers when the internal combustion engine came on the scene, all but eliminating their marketplace relevance? Or to the cruise ship industry once air travel became the preferred mode of travel for getting to Europe?

The problem is many companies don't spend enough time constructing "what if" scenarios about their future—especially if they are in situations of marketplace dominance. Back in the 1860s, for example, the railroads failed to anticipate the emergence of automobiles, which would eventually spell the end of their hegemony in the transportation industry. And in the 1980s, IBM failed to see the market moving toward PCs and away from mainframes.

There's a Hurricane Ahead

Jack Welch, CEO of General Electric, is just one of those who has sounded a warning bell that American companies today can't afford to be complacent about their prosperity and marketplace strength. This, even though the American economy has rebounded and many American executives today perceive themselves to be outpacing their foreign competitors in economic growth and expansion.

In a 1994 *Wall Street Journal* article, Welch warned of future industry consolidation and vicious battles for marketplace turf across all industries. "Things are going to get tougher. The shake-outs will be more brutal. The pace of change more rapid," he said. And then, putting things appropriately enough in meteorological terms, he went on to say that what lies ahead is "a hurricane."[11]

Perhaps, however, you think *your* industry is immune to the atmospheric turbulence in the economy today. You may, in fact, work in an industry that has enjoyed unusual marketplace stability for many years. Until recently, this was the case for the utility industry. But what if the prevailing "weather patterns" in *your* industry suddenly shifted, the way they did a few years ago in the defense industry? As one business pundit has put it, "Shift happens, so you've got to be ready for it."

No Company and No Industry Are Immune to Atmospheric Forces Today

When the Berlin Wall came down, it burst the marketing bubble that had existed in the defense industry since the end of World War II. It sent many previously successful (if complacent) defense contractors scurrying to other corners of the economy looking for customers to buy defense industry technologies originally designed to fight the Cold War.

It has taken the defense industry many years to fight its way back to profitability. Much of the industry's rebound in the United States can be chalked up to mergers among the largest aerospace players (e.g., Lockheed and Martin Marietta) and the transformation of others into purveyors of products to retail markets. Yes, weather patterns can and *do* change.

Many companies try to defend themselves against future marketplace turbulence or adverse market conditions by rushing to merge with or buy other firms. There were, for example, more than 7,000 mergers and acquisitions in this country in 1997, worth more than $650 billion. But as many as two-thirds of these efforts are destined to fail or at least fail to live up to expectations.

Why Many Change Efforts Fail

Many companies undertake change for the wrong reasons or achieve only short-term solutions at best. A company may decide to buy a smaller company with a key marketplace niche, for example, but without thinking through how the two companies' cultures can be meshed. Or a bull-headed CEO may decide to buy some company he once had a competitive dust-up with, without figuring out how such a purchase factors into the company's long-term marketing strategy.

Like Slapping Plywood Over the Windows of a Beach House

Often, mergers and acquisitions are the business equivalent of slapping plywood sheets over the windows of a beach house a few hours before a hurricane blows through. Just as the plywood sheets won't save your house from getting blown out to sea, mergers and acquisitions can't save a company that is already in trouble.

Oftentimes, these business transactions saddle a company with a hobbling amount of debt, making it worse off than it was before.

So how can your company prepare itself for change, both in the short and long term? As we'll explore in the next chapter, your organization will need to *transform* itself in some cases from the *top* down. It will need to bring in fresh executive talent, reinvent its corporate culture, or develop a new mission and strategy to help it move in new directions or respond to new marketplace realities. This need is especially true if mergers or acquisitions are to be part of the equation.

In other cases, however, successful change will mean changing things at an *operational* level. It will mean overhauling a company's management practices, redesigning core work processes, or redesigning people's jobs, to coax more productivity or efficiency out of an organization at the level where actual everyday work gets done. In still other cases, you'll need to do a combination of both.

Failing to See Micro-Changes in the Business Environment

Remember the story of the boiled frog? In it, a frog is put into a pan of water that is slowly and imperceptibly heated to the boiling point. Because the temperature change is so subtle, the frog stays in the pan and ultimately dies. By contrast, a frog put directly into a pan of boiling water will quickly jump out and save itself.

Unfortunately, many companies today become "boiled frogs" because they don't notice micro-changes in the business environment, a fact that can lead to their demise, or at least to dwindling market share and lost profits. The way to avoid this problem is to stay close to one's customers and to use information gleaned from even routine contacts with them for everything from improving core processes and business practices to developing new products and services.

Lessons from "Improvement-Driven" Organizations

That's exactly what many "improvement-driven" organizations (those that consistently improve their marketplace, financial, and operating performance) do, according to a recent PricewaterhouseCoopers' industry study. This study, which surveyed 300 companies and organizations across 15 different industry areas, found that "improvement-driven" companies have a consistently stronger customer focus than other companies do. They're also more systematic about using the "intelligence" they gather from customers (be it complaints, ideas, information about competitors, etc.) to change how they operate, to improve existing products, or, in some cases, to create new product and service offerings.[12]

A Symbiotic Relationship with the Environment

In essence, they have a kind of symbiotic relationship with their environment that permits them to continuously learn, grow, adapt, and change. Can your company say it is *this* committed to its customers? Does it treat them as the gateway to understanding the larger business environment in which it operates? Or is it like many companies that treat customers like commodities, never realizing they can be a gold mine of insights to help it position for success in a fast-changing world?

To help your company become more attuned to its environment, we've composed some questions for you. You'll note that these questions relate both to how your company interacts with the external environment and to the operating "climate" that exists inside your company.

An Organizational Diagnostic Check

Answering these questions will constitute something of a diagnostic check on how well your company is operating today. Is it in touch with its external environment? Are there mechanisms in place to forge strong links with customers? Does it appear to have the built-in capacity to change if need be? We'll take the answers you provide here and use them as part of our discussion in later chapters. This list isn't exhaustive, but it will get you started in identifying areas where your company may excel or need to improve.

Performance	Yes	No
Is your company's share price rising?		
Is market share growing?		

Is profit increasing year after year?
Is capital investment growing?
Is budget increasing? (In not-for-profit
   organizations)

Dealing with Customers and Clients   **Yes**   **No**
Is it easy for your customers to complain?
Do you have a mechanism for them to do so?
Are customer complaints looked at as
   valuable opportunities to learn?
Are complaints analyzed, tracked, and
   discussed at the most senior level?
Are changes made to work processes and
   practices as a result of customer input?
Do customers who have complained get
   redress without problems?
Is "Service to Customers" explicitly built
   into your company's mission statement?
When front-line workers deal skillfully with
   customers' concerns, is this skill rewarded?
Is your relationship with suppliers collaborative?
Is there investment in their training? Are
   long-term commitments made?
Is quality defined by what customers say
   they want, rather than by internal experts?

Alertness to Competitors   **Yes**   **No**
Is accurate information about competitors
   available to everybody in the company?
Are the strategies of competitors constantly
   scrutinized and discussed at every level in
   your organization?
Are competitors visited/studied often and their
   products analyzed?
Are the customers of competitors asked
   regularly what they think about competitors'
   products or services?

Responsiveness to Regulators/Pressure Groups   **Yes**   **No**
Is your company's relationship with regulatory
   bodies cooperative?

Has your company anticipated the policy moves
regulators are likely to make over the next
five years and made contingency plans?

Do pressure groups and unions have formal and
informal ways to represent their views at the
highest levels in your organization?

Do such groups view their relationships with
your company as effective?

Is your organization's relationship with local
and national media active and positive?

Technology	**Yes**	**No**

Has investment in technology (e.g., the
Internet) been a key component in your
company's recent success?

Do you have a detailed plan that anticipates the
impact of technological advances over the
next five years?

Is IT investment enabling your company to
have more direct and effective contact with
customers?

Does IT investment enable your company's
internal customers and suppliers to deal more
effectively with each other?

Economics	**Yes**	**No**

Is your company equipped to cope well with
changes in:
interest rates/exchange rates?
commodity prices?
its labor markets?
energy costs?
the rate of inflation?
its primary markets at home or abroad?

Gauging Nimbleness

As we said, these questions provide a starting point for understanding your company's overall operating health and the degree to which it interacts effectively with the external business environment. Depending on how many "no" answers you provide, you can arrive at a sense of how urgent it is that your company change to improve organizational performance, productivity, bottom-line profitability, or other measures of business success.

A lot of "no's" (more than six) indicates that your company may need to change in significant ways, if its future profitability (even its viability) is to be assured. There will be other question sets in other chapters, designed to help you build a profile of your organization's existing environmental nimbleness and change readiness. Let's examine now how your company can actually learn to manage change in response to changes that occur in the external business environment. After that, we'll look at a number of companies whose change efforts have (or are) positioning them for new success and business vitality in the twenty-first century.

2 Identifying the Drivers of Organizational Performance In Your Company

"Most companies don't die because they are wrong; most die because they don't commit themselves. They fritter away their momentum and their valuable resources while attempting to make a decision. The greatest danger is in standing still."

— Andy Grove, former CEO of Intel

Given the order-of-magnitude changes taking place in today's global business environment, how can your organization learn to adapt effectively in response? As we noted in Chapter 1, many companies become "boiled frogs" because they fail to note changes in the business environment with long-term implications for them. In some cases, they fail to adapt well even to changes they *do* perceive.

That's why it's so important that you see your company as a living organic entity made up of many individual components or variables, each of which can potentially be leveraged to drive transformation or renewal efforts.

Real Organizational Change Takes Place at Two Levels

For example, in the case of any organization, you have factors such as the *external environment*, *leadership*, and a company's *mission*, *strategy*, and *culture*. All these things shape and drive an organization's life in broad-gauge, "big picture" ways. Thus they play fundamental or "transformational" roles in the life of that organization. [See Figure 2.1.]

At the same time, you have variables—like a company's *structure, management practices, systems* (e.g., technology, policies, and procedures), and factors such as employee *motivation, needs, job fit*, and *work-unit climate*—all of which drive how work gets done on an actual everyday basis in the organization. These factors influence how things work at an operational, or "transactional," level.

Anybody managing change in an organization today must keep both kinds of variables in mind because each can affect the success or failure of those efforts. Moreover, when understood, they can be manipulated or harnessed to serve as drivers of organizational change and improved performance.

Is It Time for a New Identity?

Let's say that a company is trying to pursue a new business strategy, create new and better products, or get people to work more effectively together in teams. If the company has had a "command and control" culture in place for many years that has dictated people's roles and jobs, it will clearly need to change how it operates at an overall organizational, or "transformational," level. For example, the nature of the company's leadership will probably have to change, not only to empower people to work differently, but also to move the organization in new directions. The culture will have to change, too, to support new ways of working.

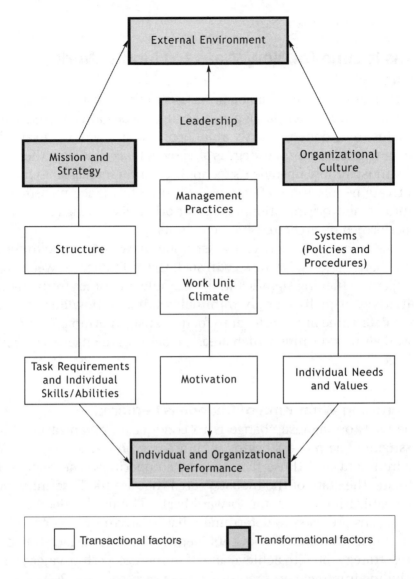

Figure 2.1 A Causal Model of Organizational Performance and Change

Source: W. Warner Burke and George H. Litwin, "A Causal Model of Organizational Performance and change" extracted from *Developing Human Resources* (Journal of Management 1992 (18) 532–545)

The "drivers" of Organizational Transformation. A company is really an organic entity. It's made up of many individual components, each of which potentially plays a role in change efforts. Factors like *leadership, organizational mission, strategy,* and *culture* shape and drive an organization's life in broad-gauge, "big picture" ways. They thus play "transformational" roles in the life of an organization. At the same time, there are variables—like a company's *structure, management practices, systems* (e.g., technology) that help people do their jobs, and factors like employee *motivation, needs, job fit,* and *work unit climate*— that influence how work gets done on an actual, everyday basis. These factors influence organizational and individual performance at a "transactional" level. Successful change requires keeping both transformational and transactional variables in mind, and using one (or a combination) of them to shape and sustain change.

Or Is It Time for New Ways to Handle Work Processes?

In other cases, however, an organization in the midst of change will have dealt with such large-gauge change issues already and what remains to be done is mostly at an operational level. For example, maybe a new business strategy is already in place, and now the company must simply upgrade its technology, train managers in how to motivate people more effectively, align performance measures to reinforce new organizational goals, or otherwise change how work is performed on an actual everyday basis.

As a change leader, you must know how and *where* to focus your change efforts. Doing so will spell the difference between your company achieving significant, measurable outcomes from change initiatives or realizing only minimal results. So how does a company determine at what level to focus transformation efforts? And how does it determine which areas to focus on to ensure its efforts succeed?

Diagnosing What Kind of Change Is Required

One way to diagnose change is to conduct an organizational assessment. The process begins with an assessment of the external environment and those factors (e.g., competitors, the regulatory climate, the state of the industry, etc.) that are likely to influence an organization on a going-forward basis. The data collected from such scans are used to determine what, if anything, the organization must "transform" about its identity (be it its leadership, culture, strategy, etc.) to achieve any of numerous performance goals, including improved profitability. (For others, see page 30.)

Once a company has done an environmental scan, an *internal* assessment follows. The goal of this assessment is to chart the dynamics inside the organization to determine how each will work for or against the change efforts planned. The data are then used to help the company create the new corporate culture, pursue the new business strategy, et cetera.

The data from organizational assessments come from at least three sources: one-on-one discussions held with an organization's top managers; in-depth interviews or focus groups with diagonal slices of employees throughout the organization; and structured surveys designed to capture and quantify responses to specific questions from large groups of employees. Information developed from all three levels of data gathering is used to diagnose what the organization needs to do to plan and implement change initiatives with a high probability of success.

Typical Questions Asked on an Assessment

What kinds of questions are asked of employees in organizational assessments? Questions typically focus on both transformational *and* transactional factors (as noted in the boxes from the top down in Figure 2.1), with questions about transformational factors being accorded greater weight than questions about transactional issues. The goal in each case is to determine the most appropriate drivers of change in that organization. Below are some sample questions.[1]

Typical Assessment Questions (Transformational Factors)

External environment. In what ways do current social, demographic, political, economic, technological, and regulatory trends impact the business? Who are the firm's current and potential competitors? Who are the company's current customers, and why do they use its products or services?

Mission and vision. To what extent are the mission, vision, and business objectives of the organization clear and understood at all levels? To what extent are major business decisions communicated in relation to the company's mission/vision?

Strategies. Is the organization competing in the right markets? How is the organization finding, winning, retaining, and developing profitable customers?

Leaders. Are leaders aligned around the vision and business strategies of the organization? In what ways do leaders communicate a sense of direction throughout the organization?

Culture. How would you describe the culture of your organization? What explicit (and implicit) characteristics— behaviors, rituals, stories, symbols, norms, and beliefs— define and reinforce a sense of culture in your organization?

Typical Organizational Assessment Questions
(Transactional Factors)

Once we've asked questions about transformational factors, we address how things work at an operational level in the organization. We ask questions in each of the following areas:

Structure. How is the organization structured? By market? Geography? Function? Process? Or is there a matrix or network form of structure?

Management practices. Are managers effective in managing and motivating others? Or do management practices act as inhibitors, keeping the organization from moving in new directions?

Systems. Do information technology (IT) systems support people in doing their work? Do policies and procedures reinforce work requirements as well as larger-gauge organizational or business goals?

Work unit climate. To what extent do people perceive teamwork, trust, recognition, and cooperation to be part of the work ethic of the organization?

Skills and job fit. Do people feel they are well-suited to their jobs, or is there a fundamental disconnect between people's skill sets and the jobs they do?

Individual needs and values. Are peoples' job growth and professional development needs (e.g., training) addressed? Or is there little in the way of a mutually beneficial employment "contract" in place to ensure job ownership and continuous skill mastery?

Motivation. Do people take pride in their work and feel a sense of commitment to the organization? Or do people feel helpless, powerless, or otherwise disconnected from the goals and vision of the organization?

Performance. Finally, do people feel they and their organization are performing at top efficiency and effectiveness? If not, then why not?

Charting the Path to Success

Once we've collected answers to all these questions and analyzed the data (using such statistical procedures as regression analysis), we can make definitive judgments about what represent key drivers of performance in the organization. Indeed, we can develop a change roadmap and help the organization's leaders understand which strategic and operational drivers of change are most appropriate to use to help them achieve their change goals.

Say that an organization's goal is to become more "customer-care oriented" in its approach to managing existing customer relationships, as in Example #1. An assessment might determine that its change roadmap calls for the following:

Example #1

Change Goal	Transformational Drivers	Transactional Drivers
Develop Reputation for High-End Customer Care	New Leadership	New Management Practices
	Major Strategy Shift Creation of New Customer Care Culture	New Performance Metrics

Or perhaps a company wants to increase innovation and shorten R&D cycles in order to become more competitive, as in Example #2. The change roadmap in this case might look something like what's pictured below.

Example #2

Change Goals	Transformational Drivers	Transactional Drivers
1. Increase Innovation	Strong Executive Support of Existing Goals	Use of IT to support team-based work approaches
2. Reduce R&D Cycle	Renewed Emphasis on a "Culture of Innovation"	Use of new training programs & technologies to accelerate learning
		Implementation of new management practices to support job redesign

The beauty of conducting change-readiness assessments is that they provide a substantive understanding of the inner workings of an organization. Once that information is analyzed, it helps delineate a clear path for an organization to take if it is to achieve successful, long-lasting change. One client of ours refers to this process as "finding the best highway" to successful transformation. Another jokingly calls it "the process of finding the yellow brick road."

As we said before, if an organization is just beginning the change process, we may determine that it should focus most of its time and energy addressing key "transformational" issues such as its mission/vision, business strategies, leadership, or culture. The solutions called for may be sweeping and require the organization to fundamentally rethink its business and organizational identity, develop (or acquire) new kinds of leaders, or radically reinvent its culture to support new business goals. This need is the case in Example #1, mentioned earlier.

On the other hand, we may determine that an organization is already well along with change efforts, and what's required now is attention to aligning management processes, business processes, technology, or people to support existing organizational goals or strategies as in the second example.

A Powerful Transformation Tool

Organizational assessments are a powerful transformation tool because they can help guide and accelerate a company toward any number of possible performance goals (internal or external). Examples of performance goals include the following:

Internal Performance Goals	*External Performance Goals*
1. Improved core competencies	1. Increased profitability
2. Increased productivity	2. Improved customer satisfaction
3. Enhanced work unit climate	3. Improved Return on Assets
4. Improved employee motivation	4. Improved Return on Capital
5. Nourishment of innovation	5. Improved market share
6. Reduced R&D time	6. Increased revenues
7. Many others	7. Many others

When to Conduct an Assessment

Conducting an organizational assessment is a logical precursor to planning and implementing any large-scale transformation effort. There are several reasons:

1. *It enables an organization's change leaders to rank, in order, how and what to change.* By analyzing assessment findings, an organization can determine which organizational "domains" to concentrate the most attention on in planning and managing change efforts. This process helps accelerate, sustain, and optimize transformation initiatives as they go forward.

2. *Unlike other change management approaches, which base change goals on anecdotal information, organizational politics, or SWAGS (scientific wild-ass guesses), change-readiness assessments are a robust research tool.* They help organizations gather concrete data about specific "identity" and "operational" change issues that can be used to build a powerful business case about why change is critical to the organization's future.

3. *Conducting an assessment sends a strong signal to employees that a company is serious about transformation efforts.* Thus it's a powerful way to combat employee apathy and skepticism; furthermore, it negates the impression that change initiatives are simply another "flavor-of-the-month" management initiative.

4. *Conducting additional assessments on a periodic basis enables you to benchmark the progress you're making in achieving real change.* Because assessments provide you with a wealth of quantitative data about the different operating zones of your organization, they enable you to gauge progress with transformation efforts over time, to pinpoint trouble spots, and to take corrective action, when necessary, to improve results or boost organizational performance.

5. *Assessment findings provide the basis for a company to create the "climate of organizational alignment" it needs to support and sustain change over the long term.*

What do we mean when we talk about "creating a climate of organizational alignment" to support change? To be successful with change over time, an organization must create the right "internal environmental conditions" to sustain success. That means eliminating obstacles, overcoming inertia, aligning systems, and otherwise creating structures to build momentum and push change forward—after the initial excitement and fanfare of a change initiative's launch has faded. As we show in subsequent chapters, today's most successful change makers instinctively realize the importance of this need.

Chapter Conclusions

Managing complex change efforts today requires a keen awareness of the factors that can influence an organization's vitality, profitability, and operating effectiveness. This chapter has outlined briefly how one can identify those variables and harness them to serve as drivers of organizational transformation. It has emphasized the importance of conducting organizational assessments as a precursor to planning and implementing change efforts and has emphasized the need to "create a climate of organizational alignment" to support and sustain change initiatives *over time.*

Doing these things is the only way to ensure success with change initiatives. As former Intel CEO Andy Grove points out, "Most organizations don't die because they are wrong; most die because they don't commit themselves. They fritter away their momentum and resources" while attempting to make decisions.

In coming chapters, we showcase numerous companies and organizations that have created effective change roadmaps using the very tools and techniques outlined in this chapter.

Each organization we profile has harnessed multiple change drivers to help drive its change efforts forward and has created a climate of alignment to sustain success for the long term.

At the start of each chapter, you'll see a graphic depicting the key organizational drivers that the organization used to leverage its change efforts. In each case, it was by focusing on these key organizational areas that the organization was able to create the "climate of alignment" necessary to drive and sustain its change efforts.

Let's look first at Royal Dutch Shell. As Chapter 3 reveals, this company is transforming itself both at a global "transformational" level and at a local "transactional" level in the more than 120 countries where it does business. By using strong leadership as well as by making changes in management practices and work behaviors, Shell is shaping fundamental changes in the company's culture. The Shell story provides an ideal case study of the kind of complex, multidimensional change efforts being initiated in large international companies today, as they respond to significant climate shifts in the global business environment.

PART TWO

The Change Makers

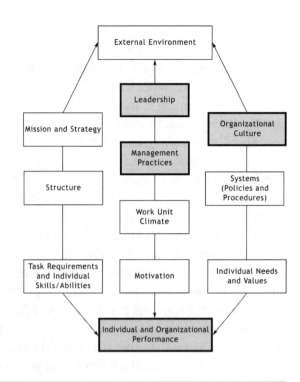

	External Environment	
Leadership		Organizational Culture
Mission and Strategy		
	Management Practices	Systems (Policies and Procedures)
Structure		
	Work Unit Climate	
Task Requirements and Individual Skills/Abilities	Motivation	Individual Needs and Values
	Individual and Organizational Performance	

3 No Simple Shell Game: How (and Why) Royal Dutch Shell is Reinventing Itself at Both the Global and Local Level

"Global organizations today find that to be successful they must stress cross-functional process more than hierarchical structure. As a result, managers are learning to look at core competencies, value-chain management, total quality management, and many other processes that are geared to marshaling the resources of the total organization to achieve business objectives."

—Stephen Rhinesmith, *A Manager's Guide to Globalization*

When it comes to market presence and global reach, few companies can compete with Royal Dutch Shell. The company operates in over 120 countries, and the Shell symbol, or pecten, is as recognizable a corporate brand as that of Coke and IBM.

Shell boasts more than 100,000 employees, manages more than 50 refineries, and controls 47,000 gas stations worldwide. It has also been extremely profitable. In 1996, the company racked up $8.9 billion in profits and since 1992 has generated an average 20 percent annual total return.

Yet the company is involved today in a massive effort to reinvent itself—at both a global and "local" level. There are several reasons for this. First, company executives are cautious about the future profitability of the oil and energy industries, and, given the recent drop in crude oil prices to just $10 a barrel (with no expectation of near-term improvement), this is a valid concern. On top of that, 1998 was not the most profitable year for the oil and energy giant, which has created a heightened sense of urgency inside Shell about how it operates.

Other reasons go back to 1994 and 1995, when two high-profile events with political and marketplace significance catapulted the company into the uncomfortable glare of the media spotlight and showed how out of touch the company was with political realities in at least two of the countries in which it operated: First, the company found itself in a delicate situation with Nigeria's military dictatorship when the government decided to execute an environmental activist who had protested against the oil industry's and Shell's environmental record in that country. Then the company got into a very public spat with the environmental group Greenpeace over the disposal of Brent Spar, an abandoned offshore oil-storage platform in the North Sea. The ensuing public relations battle became so heated that it caused Shell's profits at some German gas stations to drop by as much as 50 percent.

A Vulnerable Public Image and Bottom Line

Both events sounded a wake-up call to Shell executives and showed how vulnerable the company's public image (and bottom-line) could be if subjected to unfavorable press coverage or other public scrutiny. They pointed out that, while the company's legendary technical competence (and old-style approach to doing business) had enabled it to build oil platforms in turbulent seas and operate successfully in Fourth World countries, those successes weren't without their downsides.

About this same time, several Shell operating units also began to experience lackluster business performance. And while the company's cash reserves were enormous, the company had become complacent about efficiency and the actual cost of doing business.

Seven Out of Seven in ROI

"By the end of 1997, we were seventh out of seven oil companies in return on investment, and while we had $10 to $12 billion in cash on hand, it meant we weren't coming up with new capital opportunities for the business," says Mac McDonald, head of Leadership and Performance Operations (LEAP), a group of internal change agents at Shell charged with helping the company overhaul its corporate culture and improve bottom-line business performance.

McDonald says the previously described events—political, environmental, and financial—prompted Shell's then-CEO Cor Herkstroter to convene the first-ever conclave of senior Shell executives from across all lines of the company in 1994 for a soul-searching discussion of the business. In that meeting (and others that followed), it became clear the company needed to look hard at its cost ratios, business processes, decision-making style, and organizational culture for answers about why things were going wrong.

No Strong Commercial Capability

The urgency of reform was backed up by a review of Shell's Service Companies, which showed that company executives were remote from everyday workers, that the company's culture was insular, and that Shell's attitude toward customers was aloof if not outright dismissive. "The review showed that we lacked a strong commercial capability," says McDonald. "In our products business, we were a retail organization that didn't have much expertise in dealing with customers. In fact, we acted more like a wholesaler than a retailer."

As for the company's traditional consensus style of decision-making, the review determined that *it* wasn't serving the company's best interests, especially in a world of rapidly changing market-place and political conditions. "Over a 35-year period, Shell built up a masterful capability for a consensus style of management, even though it was usually a slow decision-making process that didn't always result in the highest-quality business decisions," says McDonald. For example, it didn't foresee the political and commercial fallout from abandoning Brent Spar. Nor did it always lead to Shell running profitable operations.

It was then that Herkstroter asked McDonald (who was then head of Shell's worldwide Contract and Procurement Group) to form an internal cadre of change agents to help transform Shell into a more efficient and customer-responsive company. "Cor came to me and said, 'We want to create an organization to accelerate the transformation process here in Shell. Would you be willing to head it?' " says McDonald.

A Vehicle to Drive Internal Change

McDonald eventually took the job, but not before laying down conditions he felt essential if LEAP were to serve as a catalyst for real change: "First I told Cor that I had to report to him. I wasn't going to report to HR because, for the program to be successful, it'd have to be driven and owned by Shell's Committee of Managing Directors (CMD), not by HR. Second, I didn't want to call it the 'Learning Center,' as he'd suggested, because that would sound too much like a headquarters-driven change initiative, rather than one that had to be owned by the business units. Third, I felt the organization needed to help Shell's various businesses produce real results if it were to be taken seriously by employees."

Thus LEAP, as an internal change group within Shell, was formed in 1996. Its mission: to serve as a vehicle through which the CMD could drive transformation throughout all of Shell's operations worldwide. To create his change team, McDonald did something novel. After forming a core group drawn from various Shell businesses, he went outside to cull additional business and facilitator talent.

"When we kicked LEAP off, there was strong feeling that we needed to bring in some outsiders, people who'd had successful business careers elsewhere and who'd have credibility," says

McDonald. Individuals with such outside experience, McDonald felt, would bring new, much-needed perspectives to how Shell had always done business and would help break down cultural resistance to change.

LEAP operates on a framework of transformation built originally on the ideas of Noel Tichy, author of *The Leadership Engine* (Harper-Business, 1997). This framework is based on three cornerstones:

1. "Leaders developing leaders"—leaders must take responsibility for transformation and for developing other leaders in the process

2. "Blending the hard and soft"—transformation programs must deliver hard business results while at the same time changing individual and team behaviors that improve the sustainability of hard results

3. "Achieving scale and speed"—transformation efforts must touch a critical mass of people in a very short period of time to overcome the natural resistance to change that exists in any organization.

Against this backdrop, LEAP today offers an array of change-management programs and services, including workshop programs in leadership development, business performance improvement, team-building, and results-and-action planning. The programs go by names such as Business Framework Implementation (BFI), Focused Results Delivery (FRD), and Shell Leadership Challenge (SLC). All are designed to build greater effectiveness and efficiency into Shell operations, to increase accountability, to improve metrics, and to create a stronger performance culture inside Shell. Above all else, though, they're intended to heighten the urgency with which Shell does business on a global basis.

LEAP operates everywhere that Shell has a corporate presence. At any given time, LEAP facilitators might be found in Austria and Spain, helping to overhaul the company's retail operations; in Oman, helping to develop a new generation of business managers; in South Africa, helping to redesign Shell's company procurement process; or somewhere in Shell's exploration and production division, helping to streamline the process by which oil gets from the ground to the gas pump. "Our goal is to accelerate transformation within this company," says McDonald.

No Performance Culture

To McDonald, doing that well means helping individual business units take more responsibility for their business results but without LEAP taking direct responsibility for what individual business units must accomplish themselves. At the time of this interview, for example, McDonald had just been asked to help one of Shell's finance groups redesign its operations as the company prepares for what's expected to be a tough business climate in the early twenty-first century.

"They wanted to have a transformation manager from LEAP help them, and I said, 'Well, that might be okay. You might in fact, want to have a person from LEAP assigned full time to help you lead the transformation. But whatever you do, don't take the focus off *you* as senior financial managers having responsibility for leading *your* transformation exercise.' "

To McDonald, the difference between LEAP being viewed as an internal facilitation force and an internal staff function is critical. "Unless a company's business leaders at the line and process level hold themselves accountable for changing how they do things, real change never results. In Shell, we've traditionally been good at getting people to work on the hard stuff—things like results, metrics, and business plans. But we haven't been successful in *sustaining* changes in how people work over the long term. We don't succeed in changing *behavior.*"

Breaking down Shell's traditional top-down organizational culture and getting people to challenge each other and work in teams are just three objectives that McDonald and his team of 40 change agents are constantly striving for in projects they facilitate. But it's a struggle at times.

Changing How People Act and Think

For example, at one recent employee event, members of Shell's committee of managing directors led employees in dancing the "Macarena." It was supposed to energize employees during a long meeting and make CMD members seem more human and approachable to the average Shell worker. "Yet, there were actually Shell employees who didn't like this," says McDonald. "They thought it undignified. Old ideas about roles die hard," he says. "Sometimes people just don't get why we're doing this stuff."

On top of that, McDonald says members of his LEAP team often serve as lightning rods for peoples' emotions when groups are trying to develop new business goals, cut costs, or just learn to interact with one another in new and more effective ways. "Facilitators get the gamut of human emotions thrown at them, including anger, surprise, and revenge. It's surprising sometimes how much push-back you get from people when you've been called in to help them deal with specific problems or redesign a key process. People tell us, 'Hey we've already been through a lot of change, don't give us more.' "

Measuring Success

Still, LEAP facilitators have received high marks for many sessions they've facilitated, such as when they helped Shell South Africa (SSA) redesign its working capital practices and implement a new enterprise-wide computer system—all to the tune of $35 million in cost reductions.

How does McDonald assess LEAP's success to date? For starters, LEAP members have conducted programs on virtually every continent and, in most Shell business units, from the retail business and exploration and production to chemicals and renewables. And the group is now getting a lot of repeat business from units. What's more, LEAP's web site records between 10,000 and 11,000 hits a month—a sure sign, McDonald says, that Shell employees have more than a passing interest in what transformation and learning are all about.

Still, McDonald thinks the onus is on LEAP to keep demonstrating its *own* results. He'd like to see 15,000 to 20,000 people go through LEAP programs each year so that they can take what they learn back to their individual Shell business units.

As far as LEAP's services are concerned, McDonald preaches the gospel of rigorous self-improvement. "Early on, we spent a lot of time developing content for our programs and putting together a new business model for how the company needed to operate," he says. "As we've gotten further along, it has become clear how inadequate we are sometimes as facilitators in broaching tough subjects and getting people to thrash through solutions to problems. It takes an experienced or gifted person to stand up and deliver content while also understanding the emotions and body language of everybody in a room."

While executives like McDonald are pushing change from a position at the center of Shell Corporate today, others are doing it at the grassroots in the many different countries where Shell operates. In no country where Shell operates are the challenges of change more daunting than in South Africa, however. There, the country itself is going through massive transformation; there's a new Constitution, a newly enfranchised market of consumers for Shell products, and a rapid rush of new entrants into the gas and energy marketplace on an almost daily basis.

Red-Flagged for Poor Performance

All that has created a context of business uncertainty and turbulence unusual even for an emerging market, and it has taken time for SSA to find its footing. This, after a 1994 business reengineering effort resulted in the company losing 10,000 man years of business experience and after the company was "red-flagged" by Shell Corporate in 1996 for poor financial performance.

That year "we delivered just 10 percent of our [business] plan, which means we were 90 percent *off* plan," says Errol Marshall, CEO of Shell South Africa. There were many reasons: weak operations, poor budget control, sluggishness in dealing with market shifts, management arrogance, and a corporate culture that rewarded people as strategic thinkers but not as effective retailers. "Over the years, Shell built up structures and mechanisms that were almost unchangeable," says Marshall.

Retail is Details

One of these was the company's performance appraisal process. "Retail is about detail, but we were punishing people for detail. If you wanted to kill someone's career in Shell, one of the best ways was to say, 'He gets very involved in detail.' So everybody tried to be a strategic thinker. If you were seen as embedded in detail, you got nowhere," says Marshall.

Thus one of Marshall's first challenges when he took over as Managing Director of SSA in January 1997 was to rally people around a common set of values and business goals and to get people focused on details. To do that, he used a unique weapon: people's sense of shame about what Shell had become.

Leveraging a Need for Pride

"People had always been proud of working for Shell, but suddenly all these bad things were being said about the organization," notes Marshall. Indeed, everyone from journalists to government officials to industry analysts had begun saying the company was washed up, that it couldn't make a profit, and that the whole culture of the company was dysfunctional. "There was this enormous feeling of shame in the organization, and people were asking themselves what had gone wrong," Marshall says. "The red-flag process gave me the crisis I needed in order to say to people, 'We can't carry on like this. We're not doing well, and I know you want to be proud of the company you work for. What are *you* going to do about it?' "

That was in January 1997. Since then, Marshall has worked to stop turf wars and battles over competing business agendas and to get employees working together, using three LEAP programs of McDonald's (Business Framework Implementation (BFI), Focused Results Delivery (FRD), and Shell Leadership Challenge (SLC)) and locally developed vision/mission workshops to do it. The goal of these programs is to train people to engage with one another, to get aligned around common objectives, and, most important, to use a common "language of change" to pursue business goals.

Forging a Common Language of Change

"Definition of words is critical to any change effort," says Marshall. "If people use different definitions for the same word, you get massive miscommunication going on in the organization." Indeed, before introducing BFI and FRD, there was massive misalignment of people and resources inside SSA. "One person's strategy was another person's action plan, which was another person's hope for the future, or statement of intent, all of which translated into people working at cross-purposes from one another," says Marshall. "We didn't have a framework or defined business direction, so individuals reacted in the only way they could: They mapped out pieces of turf and said, 'I control this.' "

As part of his leadership, Marshall had a goal of trying to help managers develop a "teachable point of view" about change that could be easily "cascaded" throughout the organization to build momentum and support for new ways of working. The concept of "teachable point of view" is the brainchild of consultant Noel

Tichy, who emphasizes the importance of creating organizational alignment around key business priorities and then generating emotional commitment to those goals.

Developing a Teachable Point of View about the Business

Today, the framework for change at SSA revolves around four key business principles: *teamwork, openness and transparency, customer focus,* and *delivery of results*—all of which represent large culture shifts for SSA.

"We spent a lot of time defining what those words meant to us," says Marshall. "For example, we've got a simple vision statement that says, 'Shell will be the customer's first choice.' It's only got seven words, but each of those seven words has fifteen minutes of teachable point of view attached to it."

As Marshall galvanized his team, however, he realized he needed more than a philosophical framework to drive change. He needed an emotional angle as well, something to energize people and give them a new sense of organizational purpose. He finally found it through the artful use of the familiar Shell symbol: the pecten.

Power of the Pecten

To *emotionally* engage SSA employees in the change process, Marshall spent time in employee meetings challenging people about what the Shell symbol meant to them. The move was calculated to transmute people's shame over what Shell had become into something new, positive, and powerful. And it worked.

"I suppose the equivalent of this would have been to desecrate a cross or something, but I held up the pecten and said to people, 'What do you think this is? This isn't the *brand*. This is just a very funny drawing of a shell. This is the manifestation of the brand in the customer's mind, but y*ou* are the brand! So let's talk about how you want customers to think about Shell. Then we can decide how you need to act so that when customers see this symbol, it has the force you want it to have.' "

A Transformational Moment

Marshall says that challenging employees to redefine what the Shell symbol meant to them personally proved to be a "transformational moment" for people. For years, the pecten had belonged to the marketing department, he says, but to nobody else. "We took the brand down off the mountain, gave it back to the people, and said, 'This is your behavior. What are you going to do to make customers feel good when they see this symbol?' People really internalized this."

That, in turn, precipitated conversations about customers and Shell's position in its marketplace. There were heated discussions, for example, about customer focus, about whether gasoline dealers were customers or whether Shell's real customers were the retail buyers at the gas pump. Together, SSA employees decided their real customers were retail buyers at the gas pump. The dealer was simply a *channel* to that buyer.

A Rapidly Shifting Customer Base

The exercise served as an important icebreaker in getting employees to focus on what they personally had to start doing if SSA were ever to show a profit again. It came none too soon since today South Africa's consumer and business markets are changing rapidly.

"One characteristic of emerging markets, whether in South Africa, Indonesia, or Thailand, is that there are enormous discrepancies in wealth," says Marshall. "In the past, here in South Africa, those discrepancies were racially dictated." Now, he says, with all the social transformation in South Africa, there are still big differences in wealth, but the mix of people with that wealth is changing rapidly. "There are entrepreneurs out there building businesses. There are new expectations. The mix of the customer base is changing in terms of spending power and new values."

That means SSA must become more nimble in dealing with different kinds of customers and must understand specific retail markets better. "Agility in understanding how our customer is changing is very important," says Marshall.

For example, personal safety and convenience are big issues in South Africa today, and Marshall sees a need for SSA to more effectively bundle the kinds of products that it sells with gasoline in some gas stations. In crime-ridden areas, for example, co-locating a convenience store or pharmacy with gas pumps could very well increase traffic flow and revenue in those places, he says, by appealing to customers' needs for safety and convenience.

We Can't Be a One-Size-Fits-All Company Anymore

But Shell South Africa doesn't have much expertise in matching convenience products (e.g., food items, toiletries, and sundries) with gasoline sales in retail markets where it operates. Indeed, the company has a "skills gap" when it comes to understanding and applying good market research, says Marshall. "We've tended to be a 'one-size-fits-all' company with a standardized product. Increasingly, however, we're finding that when you get down to the detail, you've got to think not only site by site but also customer to customer."

If reading consumer tastes is tough now, Marshall says it will get harder in the future, as wealth becomes more widely distributed throughout the country and as the typical retail consumer profile in South Africa undergoes a radical change. "I expect that, within 20 years, 70 percent of SSA revenues will come from black people because they're 70 percent of the population."

Then, of course, SSA has growing competition to think about as well, as the country moves toward deregulation. "We have new entrants coming into the market, and existing players are changing their behavior," says Marshall. To keep track of it all, Marshall and his senior management team meet regularly in what they call their "games room" to chart the emerging interrelationships among some 30 business competitors.

As if the above weren't enough to worry about, Marshall must also deal with the "people problems" that invariably arise inside a company when any kind of change is implemented. For example, learning to work in teams and to challenge their co-workers and superiors are tasks proving to be tough for many long-time SSA employees because they represent big changes in job status and how work is performed. "The new corporate value of openness and transparency is the slowest new value to take root in the organization," says Marshall.

Change Leaders Must Be Consistent in Their Behavior

So can Shell really develop the organizational skills it needs to *keep* changing on a global and local basis, as the nature of its industry, markets, and customers changes? Sustaining corporate transformation—be it on a global or local scale—is typically the most challenging part of any change initiative, says LEAP's McDonald, who notes that change leaders must be consistent in their behavior if they hope to be credible and effective with front-line workers.

"The biggest challenge we have today in Shell is to maintain our momentum, particularly in difficult economic environments where it's easy to step back and say, 'Okay, we aren't delivering on our financial targets, and part of the reason is that we're spending too much time on transformation.' We're making progress in turning the culture of Shell around from being one that didn't focus on performance to being one that delivers on its promises. But it's very easy to slip back into old habits," McDonald says.

SSA's Marshall agrees. "In any organization, people need to know that managers have a coherent story of change to tell and are consistent in what they say to people about it. The biggest benefit any leader managing change can give his organization is to be predictable, to say, 'Yes, we've got uncertainty, but the more you watch my behavior, the more you can start to anticipate my behavior. Once you do, you won't have to come to me for decisions anymore but can begin making them for yourself.' " That, says Marshall, "is when *real* employee empowerment occurs."

As for Shell South Africa sustaining the momentum *it* needs to succeed with change over time, Marshall is upbeat. He points to the ambitious goal SSA has set to achieve proportional representation of black South Africans in its management ranks by 2005. It's a huge goal for the company to reach, largely because of the talent pool of young black managers Shell must develop to fill 70 percent of new jobs created in the future.

But Marshall is confident the company can achieve it, noting that SSA started down this path before employment equity legislation became law. "We changed the rules to make this happen," he says, noting that for sometime now the company has offered mentoring and fast-track training to promising black managers and has used manager scorecards to ensure that an equitable number of black managers are promoted and developed. "If we'd simply continued with business as usual, we'd have achieved proportional representation by about 2030. But that's totally unacceptable in a country where 70 percent of the people are black."

Indeed, by moving preemptively toward proportional representation in its management ranks, SSA has shown an organizational forethought and agility not traditionally part of the old Shell culture, evidence perhaps that things really are changing at the sign of the pecten. In any event, the company is preparing for a future far different from its past, filled with more uncertainty if also greater commercial opportunity. For example, trying to anticipate what customers will want in the future (in the way of products and services) means that SSA must operate out of the box a lot of the time. "When we say, 'This is what we should be doing,' we often find customers acting differently," Marshall says.

But Marshall is upbeat even about this: "The conclusion I've drawn is that the really big business opportunities lie in paradoxes, and the thing that makes our company's transformation and our country's transformation so significant for Shell at this point in its history is that today we're not dealing with just two or three or four paradoxes. We're dealing with hundreds at a time. And in that environment, we've got no choice but to keep moving ahead."

Chapter Conclusions

What the Royal Dutch Shell transformation story reveals is that change is a complex and subtle process, especially when executives and managers must deal with a variety of factors—political, business, even environmental and social—as they undertake change efforts.

What's more, the Shell story illustrates how important it is to secure not just employee support for change but also peoples' *emotional commitment* to change goals, if transformation efforts are to succeed. "People don't work for intellectual reward, they work for emotional reward," notes Marshall. "In our case, the pecten became a powerful emotional symbol that galvanized people around new business goals and marketing priorities."

In many ways, Royal Dutch Shell today is the very model of the modern multinational. It is striving to operate nimbly both on a global basis and in a proliferating number of mature and emerging markets. Doing that well requires the utmost in leadership dexterity and, as time goes on, will require that the company nurture even greater organizational agility than it possesses today.

Shell's commitment to developing leaders at every level and to nurturing a strong internal cadre of change agents to drive continuous organizational renewal are the two cornerstones on which the company's transformation efforts rest. With this kind of "robust change infrastructure" in place, Shell stands a better chance than most companies of continuously adjusting to a changing environment. But as McDonald says, there's always the danger of a company slipping back into "old habits"—of succumbing to organizational inertia or entropy—unless a company's leaders keep the end goals of the change process forever in mind.

As we've seen in this chapter, Shell executives are more candid than many in talking about the ways their company lost its way in the past. Indeed, greater honesty and openness is emerging as one of Shell's new corporate values today.

Are executives in *your* company willing to be as candid and forthcoming about your company's business condition at this point in time? Nurturing an environment of openness and candor is critical to the successful planning of change efforts because they help break down layers of cultural insularity and management arrogance that in many cases get companies in trouble in the first place. Beyond that, planning and implementing change efforts with sufficient "speed and scale" to achieve success requires vigorous and visible top-management commitment and the ability to "cascade" responsibility for change efforts to others in the organization.

Fortunately, as this chapter has shown, the Royal Dutch Shell transformation story provides an example that virtually any company in any industry can draw lessons from as it struggles to deal with a rapidly changing business environment. For it's the story of a big company whose chastening experiences of the 1990s served as the basis for fundamental organizational learning that will serve it well in the twenty-first century.

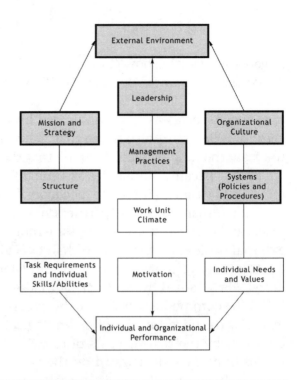

4 Only the Vigilant Survive: The SmithKline Beecham Merger Story

"Every morning in Africa, a gazelle wakes up. It must outrun the fastest lion, or it will be killed.

Every morning in Africa, a lion wakes up. It must outrun the slowest gazelle, or it will starve.

It doesn't matter whether you're a lion or a gazelle. When the sun comes up, you'd better be running."

—Unknown

When it comes to mergers, "concentrate on the marriage, not the wedding." So wrote *The Economist* in a January 1999 issue devoted largely to suggesting how companies can better make mergers work. The magazine pointed out that, in 1998, there were mergers worth $2.4 trillion worldwide (a 50% increase over 1997), including such megamerger deals as that announced by Exxon and Mobil in December 1998. But it also noted that many mergers founder and fail to create the kind of "added value" that their planners imagine.

Why? Because companies assume information technology systems will be easy to integrate, because of "questionable synergies" that make many business partners marry one another in the first place, and because many mergers are motivated more by fear of the external business environment than by a vision of the future.

"[M]any of today's [mergers] are defensive," *The Economist* noted. "Frightened by contracting markets (the defense industry), by falling commodity prices (oil), by excess capacity in key markets (cars), by the uncertainties of technological change (banks and telecoms), or by the soaring costs of research (pharmaceuticals), companies in many industries think they are more likely to prosper if they are huge than if they are merely large."[1]

The point is well taken. And it illustrates why, if a company feels compelled to grow through merger/acquisition activity (perhaps because organic growth is tough to sustain or difficult to achieve) it's critical that mergers be done right to have lasting benefit to shareholders and customers alike.

But is there a tested recipe for planning and managing a successful merger? What kind of roadmap might enable a company to avoid the pitfalls that cause so many mergers to fail or to at least fail to live up to expectations?

A Model Merger

Even today, nearly ten years after it occurred, the trans-Atlantic "merger of equals" between U.S.-based SmithKline Beckman (SKB) and British-based Beecham remains a model of what every successful merger today should look like.

Engineered by then-Beecham CEO Bob Bauman and his U.S. counterpart, Henry Wendt of SmithKline Beckman, the deal, when first announced, was given scant chance of success by many critics and business pundits and was looked upon with skepticism by investors and business journalists on both sides of the Atlantic. The American-born Bauman, a former executive with General Foods, had no previous experience in the pharmaceutical industry prior to joining Beecham. Could he become a turnaround artist? Even if that were the case, many on Wall Street and in "The City"—as London's financial district is known—questioned whether a "trans-Atlantic marriage" of two companies with vastly different cultures and personalities (to say nothing of different countries of origin) stood much chance of success. "Cross-border mergers," as they're known today, were rare back then.

Yet between 1989 (the year the merger was announced) and April 1994, when Bauman presided over his last shareholder meeting, SmithKline Beecham (SB) met or exceeded all of its business and financial targets, achieving 11 percent compound annual sales growth and 13 percent compound annual growth in both pre-tax profit and earnings per share.[2] New products launched in the same period accounted for nearly 15 percent of 1993 total sales, and that percentage was confidently expected to grow. SB's gross margin increased by nearly six points to 67 percent, and trading profit per employee nearly doubled. Sales and marketing investment showed 11 percent compound annual growth, and R&D realized 12 percent growth, reaching £575/$862 million in 1993.[3]

Discovering Secrets of Success

What are the secrets behind the SmithKline Beecham transformation story? How did these two companies with different cultures and markets manage to come together and achieve the important organizational and marketplace synergies that elude other companies? Warner worked actively with Bauman during many points in the SmithKline Beckman/Beecham integration process. He helped executives from both predecessor companies first understand their differences of approach and business style and then work together to create a new culture that would serve as the basis for creating new business values within SB.

We met with Bauman in his offices in London, where today he serves as a director of BTR SIEBE, a European consortium of engineering firms that produce automation equipment and industrial control systems. In his offices high above London's Victoria Station, he talked with conviction about what he thinks is critical to making any corporate integration effort work (strategy is critical, but even more important is good *execution*) and about what one needs to do to ensure success (get the right people on board and then instill in them ownership for the work that has to be done).

Our conversation with Bauman illuminated a roadmap that can be used by other executives to plan and implement successful change initiatives.

Before talking about the merger itself, Bob, can you describe what you found at Beecham when you assumed the helm as CEO there in 1986?

Bauman: Coming into Beecham, my first challenge was to understand where we were in the market. I wanted to know the nature of the business, what the culture was, and what the organization had been trying to accomplish as far as strategies and objectives were concerned. So I interviewed 25 or 30 top managers, plus others outside the company, including auditors and some of our major shareholders.

I asked people questions in five areas: First, I asked people what they saw as the company's *objectives*. Were they the right objectives for the company or not? Second, I asked people to describe Beecham's *strategy*. Did they think it was the right strategy for Beecham, or would they change it, and if so, how? Third, I asked people about *culture*. What was the company's culture? Was it helping the company achieve its objectives and strategies or not? And if it wasn't, how would they change it? Fourth, I asked people questions about the company's *organization*. Did the company really get organized to achieve goals, or did something need to change to make that happen? Finally, I asked people, 'What are the major issues this company needs to address, and what do you believe that I, as CEO, should be concentrating on?'

Why did you do this data-gathering?

Bauman: I wanted to become acquainted with the company's key managers and get some understanding of how they viewed strategy. But most important, I wanted to see whether everybody was thinking about these things in the same ways. Was there a clear understanding of objectives? A clear understanding of strategy?

What did you find?

Bauman: There wasn't much agreement on what the company's objectives and strategies were. In fact, there wasn't really anybody who could articulate the company's strategies. There was also a lack of understanding about the company's culture and whether or not it was important. Finally, there wasn't much consensus about where the company should be going.

Did you have other concerns that grew out of this fact-finding?

Bauman: Yes. I realized we needed to think about *people*, because we didn't have all the right people in place that we'd need to make changes in the organization and grow for the future. There was infighting too. The consumer group never talked to the pharmaceutical group and vice versa. These groups used to take turns rotating who was Chairman of the company. So there were no behaviors in place to help build the company up as it faced the future. We needed, therefore, to look at culture change.

These were pretty critical findings. They must have created a heightened sense of urgency for you because of the pressures that, at that time, were beginning to affect the pharmaceutical industry.

Bauman: Well, they did. Pharmaceutical companies had always been able to operate with huge margins, and so they could prevail in the marketplace. They had very little risk profile because their margins were so huge. Even with high R&D costs, if they got their products to market, they could still do well.

But Beecham wasn't in the top tier of drug companies. At that stage, we were down in the second 20. We really didn't have the resources to compete, so we had a choice of staying there or trying to grow bigger. Staying where we were would have made us very vulnerable. As I looked at things, the future of the pharmaceutical industry was in R&D. You had to bet your R&D. And if you had a large asset base, a large revenue base, you could place bets and afford a risk profile of having a few products not work. We didn't have that at Beecham. What's more, even though we had some promising drugs coming along in the pipeline, we didn't have the capacity to market them. Marketing is a huge expenditure. Back then it was something on the order of $100 million pounds or $150 million dollars per product.

You also had the challenge of long development cycles to deal with, didn't you?

Bauman: That, too. In the pharmaceuticals business, you have a ten-year period—at least—from the time a new drug is discovered until you bring it to the marketplace. The cost, therefore, of bringing that drug to market, as I noted a moment ago, is tremendous. Moreover, there's the risk, once you get there, that you may not be successful. Somebody else may beat you to market with the product.

Our problems weren't unlike the problems faced by airframe manufacturers who, while they have a global market for their products, nonetheless have a huge time frame to contend with, from the point at which the prototype of an airframe is introduced until it gets to market. In that business, as in pharmaceuticals, you can invest a lot of time and then find that somebody else has beaten you to the punch.

All these issues prompted us to look at how we operated and to conclude that we needed *size*—size to support our R&D, size to be able to launch products, size to successfully market them, and size to compete with the major companies.

Did you immediately think then of undertaking a merger or acquisition?

Bauman: Well, we went through the logical choices. First we asked, 'Can we grow fast enough on our own?' The answer was 'yes' if we could launch new products and have them be successful. But the problem was that everybody else was launching new products, too, and while we might catch up, it'd be hard to stay ahead of bigger players.

The second solution was to acquire. Well, that was quite expensive in those days. It still is. There are only so many companies around that are available to be bought, and, in our case, they were all smaller. We could have made a few small acquisitions. But, again, the problem was we weren't going to grow fast enough to catch up. Had we really wanted to make a major acquisition, we didn't have the capacity in terms of debt availability or resources to buy one. So that possibility was eliminated.

It was then that we looked at a 'merger of equals.' This approach avoided having to take on debt, because what you're doing is merging with an exchange of paper. You're not paying a premium. We could afford that. But it had a lot more risk profile to employees because when you put a merger of equals together, you are in effect telling employees that they are equal to the employees of the other company. It puts fear in their minds. Getting Beecham employees to come along with that was a little difficult, but eventually we got people to realize that this was the only way we could go forward.

How did you get employees to buy into that idea?

Bauman: Basically, we made the point to them that if we didn't decide to do this for ourselves and go forward with it, somebody else would come forward and decide *for* us. Remember, other companies were bigger than we were.

So, in effect, you said to employees, 'We've got to control our destinies or somebody else will,' to borrow from the title of Noel Tichy's book about his experience at GE.

Bauman: Yes. But I felt a merger of equals was a key goal for another reason. At Beecham, I was finding it difficult to bring about the kind of change I felt we needed to be successful. Change isn't easy. But a merger creates a kind of mini-crisis. Once you announce it, everyone knows that things will be different. We needed that jolt to move us forward because, remember, we weren't failing; we were doing reasonably well. We just weren't competitive going forward into the future. And we weren't growing as fast as our competitors.

So then you went out and looked for prospective partners, correct? In your book, From Promise to Performance, you talk about the process of looking at different companies. What led you to Smith-Kline Beckman?

Bauman: We needed a U.S. partner. We were strong in Europe and in most of the rest of the world, including the developing world. We had a good ability to take our businesses that were mainly in the antibiotic drug arena and move those around. The United States, though, was our weakest area, because the original patent that we'd had on a drug called amoxicillin (which was given to Bristol-Myers years back) meant that we had never achieved the same market penetration in the U.S. as elsewhere.

The U.S. was a big market, and we needed the capacity not only for R&D but also for marketing. With that in mind, we did a cross-industry analysis and came up with a list of companies. Then

I got my airplane tickets and calling cards and went visiting. Henry and I eventually met and found that we had similar visions for what we wanted our companies to be. Most important, though, SmithKline Beckman complemented our strengths, especially when it came to market presence in the U.S.

After you sealed the deal with Henry, then what? After all, the cultures of your two companies were very different. By your own assessment, Beecham's culture was commercial, competitive, and bottom-line oriented. SmithKline Beckman's tended to be rather scientific, even academic in style, and was more focused on improving people's quality of living than on the bottom-line. What did you do to align people, systems, management practices, and everybody in top management around a common set of values and goals?

Bauman: The first challenge we faced was to convince everybody in both companies that our marriage was for real, that employees on both sides were coming to it as *equals.* So we had a combined management team, made up of people from both companies, develop something we called 'The Promise of SmithKline Beecham.' We decided we all needed to own that promise if employees were to buy the message of change we were trying to communicate.

What was 'The Promise of SmithKline Beecham'?

Bauman: Basically, it was a statement that sought to capture the logic of the merger while articulating the company's higher purpose and long-term goals. The first draft of this statement was actually drafted by Henry Wendt. It said, in essence, that SmithKline Beecham wanted to be a globally capable health-care company that set the standards for the industry. We spent a weekend working together to develop that statement.

Once that was done, you felt it urgent to move quickly to sustain the momentum of that weekend meeting and transfer the energy it created to other people, right? Talk about that.

Bauman: After you craft a statement like that, your organization expects something to happen. So you have to take advantage of it. If you don't move fast, people will begin to say, 'Well, nothing has changed. Things are as they always were.' In our case, we had two companies that we'd just brought together. So it was important to change the focus from being, 'Here are two old companies. We're going to bring them together and take the best of each,' to 'We're going to create a totally new company that's able to compete in the future.'

The difference between those two things sounds subtle, but it's actually enormously important, isn't it?

Bauman: Yes. We were determined to create a *new* company, and that's what drove our work. Implementing a new culture and new strategies is the toughest part of change, and you need to involve people in making that happen and make them responsible for achieving that. So we created integrated teams bringing together SKB and Beecham managers from all over the world. These teams were set up to bring about the merger of the two organizations.

For example, in France, we had the heads of both companies work together with their key staffs to design how the *new* company would work in that region. We asked them to define strategies and plans for achieving them. Unfortunately, we didn't have a chance to get all the training in place that we would have liked to facilitate that process. So it took us longer to bring about the integration planning than we might have hoped. The upside of that, though, was that by the time these teams developed their plans, they felt ownership for the integration effort. That was critical, because, as I said before, the key to executing change is getting people in the organization to own its *implementation*.

As the teams proceeded with their work, how did you ensure that you were, in fact, creating a new company, not just a patchwork organizational design made up of individual pieces of Beecham and SmithKline Beckman?

Bauman: That's where the SmithKline Beecham promise came in. We told people, 'Hey, look, we want to stretch ourselves.' Then we put some discipline into that equation. We told people for example, 'We don't want any more than six levels between the lowest person in the company anywhere in the world and the office of the CEO.' We had this theme, in fact: 'Get the layers out.'

Second, we expected all the teams to create concrete work plans. We told people, 'Look, that work plan will be coming all the way up to the top of the organization, to the merger committee. So we want you to spell out what you see as your objectives. We want to know how you're going to measure and analyze your success in meeting those objectives.' Finally, we asked people to do benchmarking, to examine the best practices of other companies when it came to things like sales, marketing, R&D, and so forth.

Our goal in all this was to get people to step back and look around at different ways to do things, not simply to rely on their experience and habits. We used the work plans to focus people's attention and energy. And actually, the first three or four work plans we rejected. They were bad. But that got the word out pretty quickly to people that these plans were being taken seriously; they weren't just an empty exercise.

As you tasked people with developing work plans and reporting back, did you have problems or hit snags?
Bauman: There were different places where we hit snags. Some of our systems weren't able to cope with the pace of change we were trying to achieve. Getting our IT systems turned around fast enough to cope with the changes we were making was very difficult. We had one whole team that focused on nothing but how to integrate the two IT systems and how to build a supporting system.

Then there were people issues. When you're trying to manage change in any organization, you're not going to have everybody with you. Some people are resistant because they don't think you're taking the correct path. In other cases, they just don't want to change. In our case, the resistance was more in the senior-management ranks than among the younger middle-management ranks. The younger managers welcomed the opportunity that the merger presented.

Even with actively resistant people, however, I've found that you have to give them every opportunity to come along—until it becomes clear to you and especially to your organization that they're acting as roadblocks. At that point, you have to move quickly to get them out of there. If you act decisively in those moments, people will understand why. But in other cases, you can't afford to move too quickly, or you may lose people's support when you need it most. People may question your decision to remove someone rather than believe it's necessary.

That sounds a bit tricky. How do you know at what pace to lead people? When do you know if you're moving too quickly or too slowly?

Bauman: It's very hard. If you lead and find there's no one following you, you're in trouble. If you move so slowly that everyone then runs around you or behind you in different directions, you're in trouble. So getting the balance right is essential.

I think one good indicator that you're moving at the right speed is when employees *themselves* feel they're leading the change effort. Another thing you can do is to sample down through your organization and take readings on where people are. Human resources people are often a good resource to use for that. They often have a sense of how things are going. You can get good and candid feedback from them, too. Another thing is this: when you're out talking to people, listen to what people are saying. Never stop doing that.

Maybe that's a good segue into discussing the role of communications in the SmithKline Beecham story.

Bauman: Actually, I prefer to use a different word than communication for what we were doing. When we undertook the creation of the new company, I likened it to the marketing of a new brand. In this case, of course, the brand was the company. When you market a brand, you really want people to feel good about it. You want them to feel they're part of it and own it.

We weren't just trying to communicate information to people; we were trying to create a new view of what the company was about. As a result, we came up with some catchy phrases to correspond to different stages of the transformation effort. At the very beginning, for example, one of our catch phrases was 'Now We're One.' A little further into the effort, we started to use the expression, 'Simply Better.' These change slogans kept our energies focused as our efforts progressed. Actually, our communications messages kept changing as our efforts progressed and as the 'map' for managing our merger efforts evolved.

How did you go about creating a new culture in the combined company?

Bauman: The merger was just the starting point. We knew that the company would have to have a new culture. But in the beginning, we couldn't move too fast, or we would have overwhelmed both the organization and ourselves. So we began influencing the development of a new culture through the things we did and the ways we involved people in those efforts. Some people felt I moved too quickly with all this, but we all agreed that we didn't want to have an indeterminate culture that had elements of both old companies in it.

At what point did 'creating a new culture' become something you had to focus on explicitly?

Bauman: There came a time in the transition effort when I sensed we were beginning to lose what I like to call the 'magnificent energy' that pervaded the early days. As the work of the teams continued, I worried that we'd go back to what I call 'the energy of the old.'

Did you worry that efforts to form one integrated company would revert into 'camps' of Beecham and SKB employees again?

Bauman: Yes. People's energy on the teams began to lag. People stopped working as hard as they'd been working and seemed to lose focus about becoming winners as a combined company. So after a lot of discussion and debate on the executive merger committee, we decided we needed outside help to help us get clear on the culture issue and on what kind of culture we wanted to create.

That's when we brought you in, Warner, to help us first deal with our differences so that we could then move to the next stage of the integration process. You'll recall that we used the Myers-Briggs type indicator, for example, to help delineate the differences among members of the executive committee. In retrospect, that was the first step in coming together more closely as a working team.

Step two involved defining the culture we wanted. My definition of culture is that 'It's the way you work that produces a competitive advantage.' So obviously, it needed to be formed in response to external business conditions. It needed to fit our goals, our strategies, and the nature of our organization.

So the executive committee and I went away again, this time to define the values that would make up that culture. Obviously, there were certain values that were critical to our company. *Innovation,* for example, was critical. We didn't have much trouble getting people to agree on that. And by the way, we said innovation instead of 'research and development' or 'technology' because we wanted the values to be things that clearly related to *everybody* in the organization.

There was no disagreement that *customers* were critical and that our customer was changing. We weren't used to paying attention to customers as an industry because, in the past we'd had drugs, and doctors would buy them, and then patients would get them. The patient didn't know anything about them except that the doctor said, 'I'm going to give you this pill.'

But when we crafted our values, that was beginning to change. Our customer base was changing. HMOs were coming in, which brought up the question, 'Who's the buyer now, the HMO or the doctor?' and 'How do we bridge this gap?' So we knew we had to start thinking more about customers and had to do a better job— not just in providing good drugs, but also in how we managed and serviced our customers.

We extended our discussion of customers incidentally to include not just the outside world but also our own organization. Because we thought it important to say that everyone in the company has a customer. I had a customer on the Board. I had customers in dealing with members of the executive committee. We agreed that people on the manufacturing line, in R&D—people everywhere inside the company—had customers.

Another value we believed in was winning. We wanted to create a winning attitude inside the company, so we thought *performance* was important. And there was some feeling in our early discussions that we weren't driving as hard in the area of performance as we needed to.

It's worth mentioning here that different industries have different dynamics. Some industries, by their nature, are extremely oriented to getting things done. A retail operation, for example, survives on the next sale. So it's got a very short-term way of pursuing sales. When you have a pharmaceutical company that has to wait 12 years or so to get a product to the marketplace, you can get pretty complacent about losing three hours. What's three hours in 12 years? So the ideas of 'performance' and having an 'action orientation' were extremely important for us to have. We agreed we wanted to be winners and perform better than our competitors.

Another value that was clearly agreed to but harder to articulate was *people*. We knew we had to have the best people we could find and that they were key to our competitive advantage. So as part of articulating this value, we emphasized that people needed to contribute to the goals of the organization; we wanted to give everyone a chance to influence and participate in how work was done and how it got measured. And we wanted people to feel ownership for continuously improving the ways they worked on the job.

Finally, we agreed to the value of *integrity*. It's something we felt we possessed and that was important to the nature of our industry.

We felt five values was the right number. We believed that if we got too many it would be very hard to drive them all through the organization.

Once identified, how did you drive these values throughout the organization?

Bauman: After we developed the values, we rolled them down several layers in the organization. We didn't start at the factory floor, but with the top 250 managers to gain ownership from them. Through communications efforts, road shows, and other channels, the values were then taken through the rest of the organization by these managers.

You also used the power of personal example, right? As you proceeded to roll these values out, you decided it was important for members of the executive committee themselves to model the behaviors that would support these values and to be evaluated by the same measures that would subsequently be introduced throughout the organization.

Bauman: Yes. We felt that was very important. After all, the only way you really know if your values are any good is if you're willing to be evaluated on them. That helps you as a leader know they work. Second, there's nothing more powerful for the organization than to see its senior leaders and managers adhere to the same standards that are being given to others. It was key, in our minds, to creating the kind of culture we wanted at SB.

So we began using 360-degree feedback. Members of the executive committee were evaluated by their peers, subordinates, and their bosses on each of the values. It was a way to send the message that everybody would be judged in the same way and that the values we'd put in place were actually going to be used to evaluate peoples' work behaviors. I still remember that, in one case, I didn't score too well when it came to the category of rewarding and celebrating successes. I think I got a '2' out of a possible score of '5' and only got that because of my position, I'm sure. I learned from that experience, based on what people told me, that I needed to reward and celebrate successes more than I had been doing.

You bring up an interesting notion, the idea of the 'leader as learner'—somebody whose own learning provides a model for others. During the merger, you put a lot of stock in the idea of senior management team members learning new business approaches and methods that went beyond their everyday past experience. You felt so strongly about this that you took your entire executive committee to Japan for a two-week learning session with Japanese business executives. Why?

Bauman: We needed to understand the best practices of other companies and industries and find ways to apply these things to us. We had a problem on our executive committee. People had different perspectives about what we needed to do to drive change and culture through the company. To some extent, everybody had done things in other companies, and while you want diversity of thinking, people need to be aligned, and we weren't as aligned as we needed to be.

My belief is that the only way you get that commitment, that alignment from people is when they work on things together. People gain ownership of an effort *together.* The trip to Japan was intended as a way for us to come together, to test out the values and culture we wanted to bring to the company and how we could best do that. We decided to look at Japanese companies because, at the time, they had a lot of success stories to tell and because they were very willing to share what they knew with us. That surprised me at first, so I asked our Japanese hosts why they were so willing to share. They told me there were two reasons: First, they didn't believe most companies they talked to would be successful with change because they wouldn't have enough patience for the details. Second, they told me that even if we were successful, they had a five- or ten-year head start and weren't about to rest on their own laurels, so they didn't feel they had anything to fear from us.

Interesting. There was a lot of resistance to the Japan trip from people on your executive committee, wasn't there?

Bauman: Oh, yes. There was huge resistance to it inside the company. People said they couldn't afford the time. Finally, though, everybody did agree, and I think, looking back on it now, it was a watershed moment for us in trying to get people united about what we had to do. Going to Japan helped us to clarify what we needed in the way of a system, an architecture to bring our values, vision, and people together.

You've said that the trip 'lit a light bulb' inside people's heads about this. Why?

Bauman: It really did. As executive committee members met with Japanese executives and began observing how the Japanese functioned, they realized that the Japanese operated using entire management systems designed to sustain continuous improvement. Instead of the standard stovepipe functions and top-down management that most of them had known in the U.S., they saw teams of people working together closely. They saw what could be accomplished in an environment that was risk-free, where open communications helped foster a kind of collaboration and performance that was impressive, to say the least.

Gradually, I saw a paradigm shift take place, because what people were observing was process management at its best. In an industry like ours, where product push had always been the rule, people saw the power that existed when every employee was encouraged to ask what value they were providing to the customer. In my view, that was a real breakthrough for us. People came back to the States enthusiastic and convinced that they could apply the same principles in our organization.

It sounds like the trip helped people get their hands dirty with the details of organizational design. People played the role of learners and benefited by it in terms of what they then brought back to the organization.

Bauman: Very much so. People believed that the lessons of the Japan trip would clearly translate to the challenges we faced back here at that time.

That brings up another question, though, and it's this: On an operational level, what challenges does a global company like SB face when you're trying to create an integrated corporate culture across the lines of different national cultures, customs, ethnic groups, and histories? Is it possible to apply a single set of business goals or values to all employees, regardless of their background and culture, or do you need to allow for different cultural mind-sets in people, in the different regions and countries where a global company like SB operates?

Bauman: I'd answer that question this way: It's tough. When we first announced the merger of SKB and Beecham, Henry and I did road shows. He visited Beecham offices, and I went to SmithKline operations so we could meet each others' employees and they could meet us. While we found differences in different locations, we concluded that our efforts to build a single new culture for the integrated company *could* cross borders, but we had to stay focused on that.

I remember when I first came over to the U.K. from the U.S., people wanted me to talk about the differences between management styles in the U.K. and in the U.S. And I said to them, 'Look, I'm not dumb. I'm not going to talk about that. I have enough problems, thank you. Besides, we should be talking about similarities.' Because, basically, in my book, good management practices can be adopted *anywhere.*

Let me give you an example. We took our culture change efforts to all the countries where SB operates, and we didn't have difficulty implementing them anywhere. Even in France, where some people said it would never happen. They went for it—in their own way—but they went for it. China took to it very fast. So culture change contains principles that are common sense. You've got to put change principles 'in the language' of the various countries where your company operates, but basically they can and must move across borders, especially today.

Bob, as you led change efforts at SB, what did you learn personally about yourself, as a leader and a person?

Bauman: Change is hard work, and being a CEO is hard work. It's certainly the hardest thing I've ever done. When you're leading change, it's especially hard. You've got constant tradeoffs to make. You must continuously ask yourself, 'Am I going too fast or too slowly?' 'Is the organization with me or not with me?' 'Am I balancing things right or not?'

You've got other things to balance, as well. 'Am I making the right balance on investments?' 'Have I got goals appropriately balanced between short term and long term?' In my view, for example, you can probably always produce more profits in the short term, but it may be at the expense of investing long term to strengthen the organization. So you're always asking yourself these questions.

Again, it comes down to good implementation of change, doesn't it? Balancing the need to lead with the need to allow others to 'own' what they're doing.

Bauman: Absolutely. You want to involve as many people as you can in what you're doing. Insofar as the leadership issue is concerned, at some points in our transformation process, there were undoubtedly people who would have said I was a control freak or something close to it. At times I'm sure I was because I felt I had to hold people responsible for the things they'd committed to, and, besides, you can't have change efforts go off in a lot of different directions. You need discipline, and things like systems and culture give you that discipline.

Within these systems, however, you want people to own their own work as much as possible because that's where the power is. If you can delegate it down so people are in control of what they're trying to do, they'll be motivated to do their best, and that will help *you* tremendously.

Chapter Conclusions

Most so-called "mergers" aren't mergers—not really. More often than not, they are acquisitions with one of the parties gradually if not immediately taking over.

The coming together of SmithKline Beecham was a genuine merger. What made it so?

First and foremost, the merger was forged from the ground up, beginning with the crafting of a new mission and vision—the "promise"—as it was known in SB. The crafting of this statement provided the momentum and clarity of direction to spur subsequent developments leading to the birth of an entirely new company where two others had existed before.

The merger was strengthened by the creation of a new culture that provided the impetus and context for employees from both predecessor companies to come together to create an entirely new corporate entity. This proved both synergistic and salutary. Social psychology teaches us that, to resolve conflict between two parties, it's critical to have a goal that can be achieved only when both parties cooperate to reach it. The SB "promise" embodied a set of goals that required Beecham and SmithKline employees to work together, with each company bringing its inherent strengths (for SmithKline, its R&D; for Beecham, its marketing expertise) to the table. Today, this gives SB the strength of focus, organizational will, and business resilience to compete in a highly competitive health care environment.

The Beecham/SKB merger was given further impetus by the creation of a set of values to undergird its new culture and by the translation of these values into behaviors, particularly leadership behaviors. The purpose behind "translating values into behaviors" was to ensure specificity (e.g., what particular behaviors on the leader's part would help the company realize the value of, say, innovation). What's more, it created a means to measure and provide feedback on how the organization was progressing toward realizing its values. Using a multirater feedback process, leaders throughout the company (starting with Bauman's top team, as described in the interview) received feedback on how they were doing with a set of key leadership practices.

Many other learning points can be gleaned from the SB story. Clearly, for example, important momentum for the merger resulted from the work of the merger-management committee in driving the effort. The "branding" of the change effort through the use of strong and consistent communications messages unified people and gave common focus to people's work efforts. The roles that Bauman and Wendt each played had enormous influence in integrating what had been two very different companies. Finally, the team-building that occurred in Bauman's top management group as the result of its members having shared learning experiences (e.g., the Japan trip) strengthened team cohesion and, consequently, top management's role in driving this merger forward.

No Simple "Shake-and-Bake" Recipe
for Managing Change

There is no single prescription for effective leadership of change, just as there is no "shake-and-bake" recipe for managing every transformation initiative. Every leader's approach will be different based on a blend of his or her talents, temperaments, training, and experience.

This chapter has provided you with unique and powerful leadership tools that you can use to manage change based on the insights, perspectives, and track record of one highly successful change leader. In the end, *your* efforts as a change leader stand the best chance of success if you pay attention to the particulars of your situation, remain vigilant about the changes (often rapid) occurring in your company's and industry's operating environment, and shape the contours of your organization's transformation efforts in response.

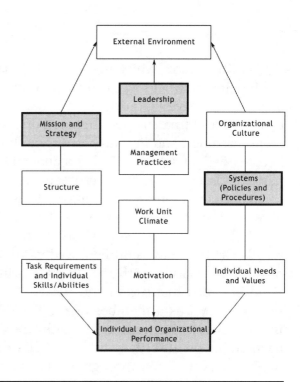

5 We Were Profitable but *Not* Competitive: The Premier Bank Reengineering Story

"There is at least one moment in the history of every company when you have to change dramatically to rise to the next performance level. Miss the moment, and you start to decline."

—Andy Grove, former CEO of Intel

Back in 1988, shortly after taking over as CEO of Premier Bank in Louisiana, Lee Griffin got what other people would have considered a distressing phone call from a prominent federal official in Washington, D.C. "Lee, I want to tell you that I've never seen a bank in the shape your bank is in that has survived," Griffin recalls the Comptroller of the Currency telling him in that conversation.

Griffin's bank, which not long before had weathered the storms of plunging oil prices and bad real-estate loans, had recently been assessed a "CAMEL" rating of "5." CAMEL ratings, which assess a bank's overall financial health based on its capital assets, management, earnings, and liquidity, are something like a "Good Housekeeping Seal of Approval" that's applied to financial institutions nationwide by the U.S. government. A CAMEL rating of "1" is considered excellent, but a rating of "5" is the worst a bank can get, akin, in some respects, to it being declared dead and buried.

"That's the way I started off my tenure as CEO of Premier," recalls Griffin today, a bit bemusedly. Yet, within just a few years of his conversation with the official, Griffin took a nearly moribund financial institution and turned it into an earnings powerhouse. Today, as a member of the Bank One family of banking institutions (with a new name, Bank One of Louisiana), Premier is a vibrant corporate citizen not only in Baton Rouge, where Premier Bank had its start, but throughout the entire state of Louisiana and beyond.

What was Griffin's recipe for turning Premier around? How did he bring his bank back from the brink, after it was all but declared dead by traditional standards of financial performance in the banking industry? As this chapter shows, it isn't because Griffin is a charismatic leader with the oratorical gifts of Ronald Reagan (although he's quietly persuasive and connects well with people); nor is it because all of Premier Bank's business problems suddenly evaporated when Griffin assumed the CEO role in 1988.

It was because this slim and soft-spoken Southern gentleman, whose Baton Rouge office overlooks a sprawling Mississippi, knew how to effectively tap the best in his employees, and because his hands-on leadership style made him a credible (and well-liked) agent of change within an institution bound by strong banking traditions. Then, too, it was because Griffin knew how to appeal to employees' loyalties and desires about the future of Premier as an institution, even though, as part of transformation efforts, he didn't guarantee future job security to anybody. But ask Lee Griffin himself what he thinks made the difference in Premier's transformation success, and he'll say something else: "During times of change, you must communicate with employees and demonstrate you care about them. No two things are more important to your success than that."

Indeed, both these themes run broadly through the transformation efforts that Griffin initiated inside Premier in 1993, after he'd brought the bank back from the edge of the cliff but at a point when the bank's future financial health was still anything but assured.

Performance Indicators Foreshadowed Problems

"At that point we were very profitable, but we still weren't very competitive," recalls Griffin now. While bank profits were up, other performance indicators foreshadowed problems. The bank's efficiency and performance, as measured in "assets per employee" and "revenue per employee" ranked near the bottom in its market and against various peer institutions.

At the same time, Premier was trying to shift commercial gears. Though traditionally a brick-and-mortar operation, where loan officers knew customers by name and friends caught up with each other while doing business over varnished oak desks and polished marble countertops, market research showed the needs and tastes of Louisiana bank customers were changing. ATMs were very popular, and telephone and online banking were in their infancy. And while the bank's older customers were a sure bet to keep using Premier's network of 150 or so bank branches to conduct business, other customers (young families, singles, professionals, and dual-income couples) were demanding greater speed, convenience, and variety in banking services

All this convinced Griffin and his top management team that they needed to reengineer the bank's operations to become more customer-responsive and to stay ahead of changing customer demographics and banking habits. Their redesign efforts had to produce enhanced customer service for the bank, increase the speed with which services were provided to customers, and cut costs dramatically. To be successful, they would need the support of all bank employees, some of whom would lose their jobs in the reengineering process.

Engaging the Hearts and Minds of Employees

Mindful of the short-lived success of many corporate change initiatives and the outright failure of others (a recent CSC Index survey had indicated to him that approximately two-thirds of all reengineering efforts are clear busts), Griffin realized he couldn't just mandate change in his organization. He had to engage the hearts and minds of Premier employees as part of the change campaign, even though in some cases it would spell the end of years of job security for those very same employees.

How did Griffin do that? In his mind, it involved six critical steps, which, when systematically planned and implemented, helped build momentum for change inside the bank. They also created a "climate of organizational alignment" to sustain those changes over time.

Step 1: Get Agreement at the Top About What You're Going to Do

"First, we needed to get agreement at the top of our organization about the changes we were going to make," says Griffin. At Premier, top-level executives came to a consensus about the new directions that the bank needed to take after Griffin held a series of executive-level workshops. These workshops developed a new mission, vision, and set of values for the organization and established aggressive, measurable objectives for the reengineering initiative.

Out of these workshops came an awareness that Premier needed to continue leveraging high-quality customer service as a "primary differentiator" in the Louisiana marketplace. But bank executives also agreed, after some heated discussion, that the bank needed to lessen its traditional reliance on branch banking and rely more on technology as the way to deliver an increasingly sophisticated array of bank products and services.

So they decided to reengineer four key bank processes: consumer lending, commercial lending, new accounts, and back-office transactions. Even before the workshops, "we knew customers were demanding greater speed, convenience, and variety of bank services and products, which automation could in fact help us deliver," says Griffin. But it wasn't until bank executives held strategy sessions (using electronic meeting technology called "groupware" to help them thrash through differences of opinion) that an actual group consensus emerged, both about the use of the technology and the urgency of doing so.

To some banks that have been technology-driven in their delivery of bank services for years, this may have seemed like a "no-brainer," acknowledges Griffin. "But to an institution like Premier back then, which had traditionally relied on 'friendly faces and warm handshakes' to sell bank services, the idea of using lots of 'impersonal technology' to let people check their bank balances at midnight, switch money from one account to another, or secure a loan by phone (without meeting somebody face to face) had not seemed immediately like the path to take." Indeed, at the time, it seemed counter to Premier's culture of hands-on customer service. Ultimately, however, it became clear that technology would only improve the bank's ability to provide high levels of customer service.

Step 2: Engage the Arms, Legs, Brains, and Hearts of Your Employees to Help You Implement Your Reengineering Efforts

Once Premier executives and managers had determined which business processes to redesign and by which performance metrics they wanted each process measured, they put business process redesign (BPR) teams together and let them swarm across the organization. Their goals: to analyze how to improve and streamline each bank process and achieve desired improvements in performance.

Getting Down to Granular Details

As team members got down into the "granular detail" of examining individual business processes and then worked to redesign them at a "transactional" level in the bank (where actual, everyday work got done), their efforts hit pay dirt almost immediately. They were able to identify inefficiencies, troubleshoot problems, pool their thinking to creatively revamp the way things should work, and, from there, send recommendations up to an executive steering committee about how to change things, says Griffin.

Griffin says the very act of getting their hands dirty with reengineering work enabled BPR team members to feel a tremendous amount of personal ownership for what they were doing. It also made team members zealous advocates of continuous improvement. The teams worked diligently to unearth inefficiencies, mostly by asking themselves hard-and-searching questions.

"They got into rooms and had paper all over the walls, with flowcharts showing how pieces of paper flowed through the bank," says Griffin. "Then they asked themselves questions like, 'What does this step really add?' 'Can we do away with this step and actually come out with as good or a better product?' 'Can we do things faster?' 'Can we eliminate some positions?' 'What are we doing in the name of security?' and 'What audit trails are we generating that really don't make any difference to our performance?' "

People Got Energized

Griffin says the exercise of looking closely at some of the bank's most important processes not only energized employees for reengineering tasks but also showed how inefficient (and costly) some operations were and how much the institution had to change if it were to be more flexible and nimble in dealing with customers in the future. "We found that, over the years, following examination by outside examiners, internal auditors, and the like, that we'd piled so many restraints on our people that we were probably spending fifty cents to keep from losing two cents in some cases," says Griffin.

Moreover, in many cases, these process reviews unearthed "artifact" tasks and process steps that had resulted from many generations of management directing how work was accomplished. Notes Griffin: "I've found over the course of my banking career that, in any department, you normally have about three supervisors or managers over a ten-year period. Each of them initiates things within that department that are intended to improve a process during their watch. But at the end of ten years, you often have remnants of things left over from what the different managers did in the past that, in many cases, provide no value-added benefit today."

One thing that helped process redesign efforts proceed was Griffin's exhortation to his employees to leave no stone unturned in the quest to improve operations. Indeed, Griffin challenged BPR teams to root out inefficiencies anywhere they could find them. "They didn't have to worry about me jumping down their throats because they criticized the bank that I was CEO of," he says. "As they proceeded to identify problems, I simply said, 'Go for it! Let's find all the inefficiencies we can.' "

No Sacred Cows, Please

Indeed, as one member of the team that redesigned the consumer-lending process recalls: "We were told we should look for every possible way to improve efficiency, no sacred cows would be spared. Our team put this to the test when we suggested major changes in the bank card center, which Mr. Griffin had started and in which he had had an obvious continuing interest. When our recommendations were accepted, we knew top management meant what it said!"

In another case, Griffin was relentless when it came to streamlining the commercial loan approval process. When members of one BPR team told him there was no way the process could be shortened to anything less than three or four days, he told them, "No way. This has got to be done within 24 hours." If it could be done in that short a period of time, Griffin argued, customers would talk about it on the streets, and people would say, "This bank really knows how to deliver."

Step 3: Communicate the Urgency of Change

Other things that speeded Premier's reengineering efforts were Griffin's intense commitment to communicating the importance of change to employees and his willingness to serve as a sounding board (or lightning rod) for people's questions and concerns when they arose.

A Campaign of Cascading Communications

Griffin and his top management team put a plan in place to "cascade" the specifics of change implementation throughout all levels of the bank. At the heart of this campaign was the urgency of communicating to bank employees the need for Premier to change how it operated. For though profits were up, Griffin knew that many of the success indicators by which current bank profits were measured (e.g., the success with which the bank was selling off non-performing assets) were not sustainable metrics over the long term. Therefore, the bank needed to root out unnecessary costs and operate much more efficiently.

Griffin himself acted as the chief champion of change, talking to employees about it as much as possible. He crisscrossed the state for a long series of coffees with bank employees at all levels, using the opportunity in each instance to answer questions, address concerns, even deal with hostile questions, such as when an assistant vice president in one bank office asked him how the bank's board of directors could possibly justify paying him the salary it did.

"To tell you the truth, that question threw me a bit," says Griffin, noting that he apparently diffused the woman's concern after being open to hearing her voice her views. And lest anyone think that she might have ended her upward mobility in the bank with that question, Griffin says, quite the opposite occurred. Six months later, the woman had been promoted to a VP-level job.

As for how he addressed the issue of job security as operating efficiencies were identified and then implemented in the bank, Griffin offers this: "People can lose their jobs because a company is ineffective and your competition beats you down to a nub. They can lose their jobs because of mergers and acquisitions, and they can lose their jobs because of processes being redesigned," he says. "But at the end of the day, I always told employees that what the bank needed were people committed to being winners." He believes people bought the urgency and reasonableness of that argument.

Being Frank but Showing You Care

"As part of our reengineering efforts, we invested $17 million in new hardware and software, and I told people that you can't invest $17 million in new technology and not cut costs somewhere. We could have layered the cost of new technology onto what we were doing, and it might have helped the customer. But we wouldn't have been doing a very good job for shareholders, and I told people that." Still, Griffin believes, people realized that he cared deeply for those bank employees who would likely lose their jobs as the result of restructuring.

"As we went through reengineering, everybody knew that they'd have to sacrifice some people that they didn't want to lose out of their workflow," he says. But when people recognized that others around them were sacrificing, as well, and that the bank really had to hang on to the very best and most appropriate bank employees, people understood what we were trying to do."

Nonetheless, Griffin made it clear to every bank employee he encountered that, even if the bank wound up eliminating their jobs or the jobs of others, he'd do everything he could to make sure they landed a job somewhere else or benefited from the most generous outplacement packages he could deliver.

Step 4: Put Yourself in the Shoes of the Front-Line Employee

Still another thing that built employee commitment to change, Griffin believes, was when he put himself in the shoes of front-line employees, something he did quite visibly one time when he spent three days working on a teller line. "I hadn't been on the teller line since I first came with the bank more than 30 years ago," he says. "But I went to our operations center and started working the various clerical desks so I could find out what our people there were actually going through, what kinds of challenges they faced each day, what kinds of inquiries and complaints they had to deal with, and what made their jobs difficult."

Griffin believes it made a difference to his reengineering project's success that he came out and took his turn working a teller window. "I think it counts when a CEO does something like that. It shows you care, and people pay attention to that, especially when you're asking new things of them."

As a Leader, Be a Learner

Griffin says working the teller window after an absence of several decades was also a *learning* experience. "I tell you, I was not a very good teller," he jokes. "I had to ask a lot of questions, because I found out that being a teller today is far different from what it was back in the 1960s. There are so many more products and services. You've got to be a psychologist, a salesperson, a mathematician. You've got to understand technology. And all that has to be brought together in a few seconds when a customer is sitting in front of you asking you to complete their transaction."

Griffin thinks the fact that he worked the teller line telegraphed a message to employees that he not only cared about them, but also considered himself one of them. Establishing that kind of solidarity with employees is *critical* during a change effort, he says.

"I'd recommend that any CEO spend 50 percent of their time with employees or customers. As far as I'm concerned, if a CEO doesn't do that, they're not doing their job."

You've Got to Keep Your Ear to the Ground

Griffin says there are still other reasons to spend time with employees, especially during periods of transition. Having your "ear to the ground" at the business front lines affords tremendous benefits when you're trying to do something difficult like manage culture change and communicate a new business strategy to people, he says. You get unfiltered feedback, which helps you build good rapport with people. And it gives you insights into what people are thinking, which is critical when you're nudging employees to embrace new ways of working, give up old habits and beliefs, or deal with customers differently.

"Sometimes I'd do coffees with Vice Presidents, sometimes with assistant VPs, and sometimes non-officers only. I'd get the most honest answers and questions from the non-officers," Griffin admits. "If you get down with the rank and file, they'll tell you that they really, really don't like that tie you're wearing. You'd never see a vice president say that, but a teller will, and those people are where the action is. They interface with the customer every day, so I want to know what's on their minds!"

Step 5: To Be Credible as a Change Leader, Be Consistent With People

People form the foundation of any successful change effort, says Griffin. And while Premier had never done layoffs before, reengineering clearly called for it to happen. "We reduced our overall work force by 25 percent by the time everything was said and done," he says.

To deal with this, Premier made it a policy early on to tell employees that, in some cases, jobs would be eliminated. At the same time, it offered generous separation packages, including outplacement services, to support people who were likely candidates to have their jobs eliminated by the reengineering effort.

In some cases, job elimination extended even to members of the BPR teams. As one team member recalls, "In our team, we wound up considering the elimination of about half of our own jobs. We'd be working along at a theoretical level, and suddenly somebody would say, 'Hey, we're talking about Joe' or 'We're talking about me.' Team members whose jobs were eliminated recognized that a better process required a different approach. And in many cases, people whose jobs were cut had the chance to be retrained for new jobs."

Firing a Dear Friend

The consistency with which the job-elimination rule was applied extended even to Griffin's closest friends at Premier Bank, including a member of the bank's senior management team. "I had to eliminate the position of a person I loved," says Griffin. "I'd worked with him for 25 years, but everybody in the bank knew that he wasn't pulling his weight. He kind of knew it, too. I didn't have the heart to eliminate his job, but in the end, reengineering made me sit back and say, 'Hey, that's not honest.' So in the end, his was one of the biggest jobs we cut."

Step 6: Recognize That Change Leadership Is Often Very Personal

What *else* does Griffin think is crucial in successfully managing a major change effort? Well, for one thing, he says, you don't have to be a genius to run a successful transformation effort. In fact, you don't want to make things too complicated. It's more important to be straightforward with people.

"I don't pretend to be a rocket scientist or a member of the Mensa society, as my brother is. But I do care about people," Griffin says in a way that makes it clear he's as smart as a whip about people. "Even though we had layoffs to do and jobs to cut, you have to demonstrate care for employees and their lives. I don't care how good your reengineering plan is or how good your communications are, if you really don't care about people, it shows through. If employees think that management really doesn't care about their lives, their families, and their futures, employees will be looking over their shoulders every day trying to figure out how they can do something for themselves instead of for the company."

Your Company Needs Employees' Loyalty

In this era of widespread downsizings, continuous market consolidation (in industries such as banking), and the end of the traditional "employment contract" of years past, Griffin still believes there's a big place for employee loyalty in organizations today. And for loyalty on the part of an organization to its employees.

"I've read and heard many people say that, nowadays, loyalty to an organization doesn't make any difference to an organization's success. But I don't think you can build a great company unless you have loyal people who are willing to put themselves on the line—in a sense to die—for their company," he says, figuratively speaking of course.

As for a company's character, Griffin says, the way a company treats people who leave because of downsizing or reengineering speaks volumes. If people who leave aren't treated right, those who remain invariably take notice. "When we reengineered, we spent a lot of money on outplacement services and change management," says Griffin. Not only was this the right thing to do in Griffin's mind, but it also sent a message to surviving employees at a time when the bank needed them, their loyalty, and their skills more than ever. "We didn't want those who stayed to fear the future or be afraid of what change might mean for them."

One Pant Leg at a Time

So how does Griffin assess his own personal style as a leader? More than anything else, he considers himself a "hands-on" CEO who enjoys spending time with his bank's rank-and-file employees. Indeed, he sees a big need for bankers like himself and for business executives in other industries to avoid the executive suite as much as possible in order to be on the front lines with everyday employees.

It's a philosophy that Griffin still brings to his job today, as CEO of Bank One of Louisiana. "I go out to all our markets as often as I can. You have to visit with officers and directors, of course. But what I really enjoy doing is just breaking away from that to go walking around, meeting tellers and other employees, introducing myself to people, and letting them know who I am. I like to have my coat off when I do that. You can't talk family to every person you walk up to. After all, we have 6,000 employees in the state, but sometimes, when you're in a place like Alexandria, Louisiana, where we have four or five people, I'll stop to talk to somebody in a teller line or to the new accounts representative. Doing that kind of thing helps people know that you put your pants on one leg at a time, just like they do."

This same hands-on strategy is what Griffin used recently as Bank One of Louisiana completed its acquisition of First Commerce Bank in Louisiana. Griffin made it a point to spend time with First Commerce employees, even as the acquisition process was underway. And when it came time to appoint executives to head various bank operations within the Baton Rouge area, a number of First Commerce bank managers got the nod for jobs even though a number of Bank One employees might have seemed more likely candidates, given their own bank's position as the acquiring institution.

We Must Humanize Business and Create Community in Organizations

Griffin says that one of the most important things any executive managing change today can do is to recognize how much it affects employees on both a personal and job level. Doing that, he says, can build the kind of workplace loyalty and sense of community that has to exist inside a company if people are to operate at their best. "I think we have to humanize business today. If we don't do that, people won't feel like they're part of a team or a family. And they won't be willing to make any sacrifices if they think everything is run out of an ivory tower and that nobody is interested in them as people."

Chapter Conclusions

What leadership lessons can be drawn from Lee Griffin and his experiences as CEO, both of Premier Bank and now of Bank One of Louisiana? In a word, this: much of what effective leadership is about is personal, hands-on, and informal. It's as much (if not more) about managing people as it is about bottom-line business results. And it's about being a visible and empowering leader who takes a personal role in driving change efforts.

As you've seen from this interview, Lee Griffin is an accessible leader who eschews the pedestal in favor of mingling with front-line employees as much as he can. He's also good at charting an overall direction for change, building a guiding coalition to support it, and staying the course. Finally, Griffin is the kind of change leader who is able to make tough decisions and who gets out in front of people to communicate the reasons for his decisions, even while showing concern for people's welfare.

Much of what effective change management is about is persistence, says Griffin, be it personal perseverance and consistency on the part of a leader or in the structure and systems that a company puts in place to reinforce the goals of its change efforts.

Creating an Infrastructure to Sustain New Ways of Working

And it's about one more thing. In our ongoing research with clients over the years, we've found that organizations that are really good at change are, as we put it, "improvement-driven." Which is to say they are consistent when it comes to reinforcing new employee behaviors, work values, and priorities.

They make it a point, for example, to incorporate quality improvement accomplishments into people's annual performance reviews and to reinforce the importance of people taking personal responsibility for continuous improvement efforts on the job. They also go out of their way to affirm the importance of change as a corporate value and virtue, at the level of organization-wide messages to employees and in the management practices used by managers with their subordinates.

At Premier Bank, Griffin and his senior management team strove to do these things each and every day. They took pains to affirm the importance of the BPR teams, to honor those selected for membership on them, and to recognize team efforts that lead to tangible savings and improvements in workplace productivity and corporate profitability.

Griffin and company also worked to empower (with resources and top management backing) individual change "sponsors" and "champions" in the organization who helped make things happen, whether it involved streamlining the loan approval process, expediting credit approvals, reducing the amount of paperwork involved in creating new accounts, or helping bring Premier's products and services to shopping malls and workplaces, as well as to bank branches.

The bank also implemented a team-based incentive program and put new emphasis on customer service, responsiveness, efficiency, and cost savings. All these things helped to build the necessary "infrastructure" to sustain change at Premier over the long term and ultimately paved the way for its successful acquisition by Bank One.

Still other learnings can be drawn from Lee Griffin's leadership of change. For example:

- **During corporate transformation efforts, pay attention to the messages you send to employees.** Showing care and compassion for people is critical to building employee support for change efforts, even as you are asking new things of employees. If employees don't perceive you as caring about them as people, chances are good that your change efforts will fail or will fail to realize the full financial and organizational benefits that you initially envision.

- **Build employee ownership for change efforts by involving employees in transformation efforts.** This step helps build strong linkages between the jobs that people do every day and the large-gauge business goals of the organization. It helps to build the momentum for change that your organization requires if new ways of working and operating are to be sustained over the long term. One way Griffin was able to build employee ownership of change was by being a good storyteller and by providing a bridge from what the bank had been in the past to what it could be in the future. Those qualities proved to be important glue in binding employees together to support Premier's transformation efforts.

- **Don't just strive for cost savings from reengineering efforts; instead, have bolder and loftier goals in mind—especially when it comes to serving customers.** Griffin says when you're reengineering a company, you have to improve processes, empower people, and create a better organization, not just think about cutting costs. So be clear in your head about *how* reengineering will help your company serve customers better, build organizational resilience, or help you become a world-class customer-service operation. As Griffin points out, "You want people to say, after they deal with your company, 'Boy, those people really know what they're doing!'"

- **Recognize that reengineering is a process, not an event**. Reengineering initiatives don't get realized overnight. They take time. They produce results only when individual employees, working together as a team, take personal responsibility and ownership for the work they do and clearly understand how their own day-to-day jobs help support the large-gauge goals of an organization.

- **To be an effective change leader, you must lead with integrity**. You must be able to make tough decisions that affect people and be willing to defend the rationale of those decisions by connecting directly with people to do it.

If your company can manage change using the principles and ideas outlined in this chapter, you will increase the likelihood of realizing long-term success from your reengineering efforts. That's because you will effectively engage your employees, not just as cheerleaders of change, wishing you well from the sidelines, but as committed advocates and sponsors of change efforts from inside the organization.

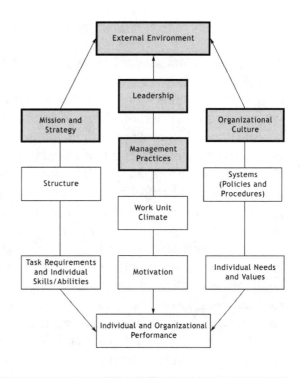

6 Plane Talk About Change: How Lord Colin Marshall Transformed British Airways Into a Customer-Service Powerhouse

"Today, leaders take nothing for granted. They know that the greater their market share and their margins, the harder other people are working to take it away from them. Their only hope is to try to discern winds of change in the market, to come up with new and improved products and services, and to try to stay two or three steps ahead of the intense competition."

—Larry Bossidy, CEO, AlliedSignal

Talk to Colin Marshall, chairman of British Airways (BA), and you soon enough discover the origins of his passion for providing customer service. Years ago, long before he transformed British Airways from a tired, demoralized, and state-subsidized air carrier into one of the world's most profitable and successful airlines, Marshall worked as a cadet purser aboard Britain's Orient Line. For much of the 1950s he served as a well-scrubbed and earnest young sailor aboard many of Britain's most esteemed old ocean liners, as they plied the seas from England and Australia to Africa, New Zealand, and the west coasts of Canada and North America.

It was years before jet travel was to become common. Ocean liners were the dominant form of trans-Atlantic travel, and Marshall still vividly recalls setting to sea for long periods of time with as many as 1,500 passengers and crew, who lived together for anything from four to five weeks at a time.

It was hardly "The Love Boat" or a Carnival Cruise. The routes Marshall worked took him through stormy seas and steamy climes much of the time—without the amenities we associate today with ocean cruising and, in many cases, even without rudimentary air conditioning.

A Formative Experience

Still, those years at sea were, in Marshall's words, a "formative experience." They taught him a lot about the nature of a service business. Moreover, they forged in him strong convictions about customer service, beliefs that later undergirded his transformation efforts at BA in the '80s after Britain's then–Prime Minister Margaret Thatcher told the airline it would be privatized if it delivered three consecutive years of profit.

Needless to say, it did. And today, thanks to Marshall's leadership, British Airways is a world-class airline with a global reach, a reputation for service innovation, and a strong brand identity. BA's marketing and business strategies, which rely heavily on promoting the BA "brand," have been highly successful in drawing to the airline a loyal and enthusiastic base of leisure and business travelers, helping the airline to compete successfully, year after year, in one of the most cut-throat businesses that exists.

BA regularly "relaunches" its airline services based on data it gleans from customer surveys and focus groups. The company plowed new ground in the airline industry in 1997, when it began offering first-class passengers "flying beds" and individual in-flight cabins. And today it's experimenting with other exotic customer amenities including on-board gambling and high-tech baggage labels to speed up the delivery of passenger luggage.

Both Warner and PricewaterhouseCoopers Consulting have worked extensively with British Airways over the years as the company transformed itself from a state-subsidized air carrier into a profit-making enterprise. We met with Colin Marshall in his office in London's Berkeley Square, just steps from the teeming streets of Piccadilly and Mayfair. Our conversation focused on how Marshall—first as CEO of British Airways and later as Chairman—successfully transformed BA's culture from one that was "engineering focused" into one that was "marketing focused."

Colin, you've described your job as a cadet purser as being a very formative experience in your life as a young man and one that helped influence your views about customer service. What made it so special?

Marshall: I worked for the Orient Line very soon after the second World War. It was less than six years after the end of World War II, in fact, and, in this country, we were still subject to food rationing and other restrictions. For me, therefore, the opportunity to break out of a rather utilitarian existence here in the United Kingdom and go to sea was quite appealing. My purser's job enabled me not only to travel to various parts of the world, but gave me the chance to meet all sorts of people of all colors, creeds, religions, and nationalities. It was like getting into the University of Life at a relatively young age.

The responsibility of the purser's department on the ships for which I worked incorporated everything other than the ship's steering and navigation. We were responsible for the catering, entertainment, and all arrangements whenever the ship was going into port. We handled the allocation of staterooms and cabins, and we were responsible for the crew's pay and rations. So I learned at a tender age about the need to accommodate people, their wishes, and their requirements because the purser's department was the focal point of the ship as far as the passengers were concerned and, to some extent, from the crew's standpoint, as well.

*After you left the Orient Line, you built on your experiences in cus-
tomer service by holding senior positions at Hertz and Avis before
coming to BA in 1983. When you came here, what did you find
lacking? What in your mind needed to change?*

Marshall: When I came to BA, I'd had the good fortune of being a
frequent commercial user of British Airways services for many
years. For the ten years from 1971 to 1981 that I lived in the New
York area and was with Avis, first as Executive Vice President and
Chief Operating Officer, then as President and CEO, I was a frequent commuter across the Atlantic to London. In those days, Avis
had its head offices for everywhere outside the Western hemisphere in London. So I used to be over in London eight, nine, or ten
times a year, and most of the time I flew on British Airways and its
predecessor companies.

I knew that passengers didn't get much service. I knew it not
only from my own experience, but because I heard others talk about
it, as well. The most serious thing I observed, though, was the low
morale among employees. Passengers experienced airline employees as really lacking in enthusiasm for their jobs. There was very little research being done at the time about what customers really
wanted, and this was clearly evident in the style of service people
received, which was abrupt, even gruff. To some extent, it showed
in the way food was presented, as well. It showed also in the fact
that the airline focused more on operations than on marketing.

How so?

Marshall: The airline focused more on operating aircraft and determining schedules and destinations for flights than on determining
whether schedules were convenient for passengers or went to destinations they wanted. Perhaps none of that was surprising because
the company was a nationalized industry at that time, and many
people working in it had come out of the military services. In any
case, there was a lack of focus on the marketplace. Indeed, there
was only one person in the entire company anywhere in the world
with the word "marketing" in their title.

Really?

Marshall: Yes. We had a Vice President of Marketing in the United
States, but there wasn't one here in the U.K. We had a Commercial

Director, but no Marketing Director. And there was no marketing department. So when I arrived, I got hold of the man (Jim Harris) who headed up the commercial side of the business at the time, the man who, in fact, had been the Vice President of Marketing in the U.S.

I told him, 'Jim, I want you to be our Director of Marketing. But before I confirm that, I want you to select four of the best younger managers in the organization who you believe can be the nucleus of a marketing department. I want you to get these people thinking and creating new marketing concepts and ideas that we can use to pull ourselves up by our bootstraps and present a far better image to the marketplace.'

In a couple of weeks, Jim came back to me with the names of four people, each of whom I interviewed and who seemed to fill the bill in terms of what I was looking for. With those people, we put together a team headed by Jim as the Marketing Director. Those people all went on to do other very successful things, and, over the years, we lost all of them, but for very good reasons. They were hired away to better positions in other organizations based on what they accomplished here.

With that team, did you flesh out a new product line and begin emphasizing the BA 'brand'?

Marshall: Exactly. There were two things we needed to address rapidly. First, we had to develop new ideas and concepts for service and get that information out into the marketplace via new forms of advertising and promotion. Second, we had to raise morale in the BA organization. We needed to change how people thought about their jobs. We needed to shift them toward customers and away from simply the mechanics and engineering of running an airline.

How did you do that?

Marshall: First, we put together customer focus groups and brought groups of customers together. We sat them down and asked them what their perceptions were of our service, our product, and what they wanted from us as an airline. We involved them to the fullest extent possible in testing new marketing concepts.

The first significant thing that came out of that effort was something we called at the time 'Super Shuttle,' which connected London with three other cities in the U.K. (Manchester, England;

Glasgow and Edinburgh, Scotland) and which we put in place about seven months after I came into the company. We provided hot breakfasts, gave people newspapers, instituted preassigned seating, which customers paid for before they got on board, and had backup aircraft available in case they were needed, as well. Doing all this was quite extraordinary at the time.

Before this, we'd had a shuttle, comparable to the old Eastern Airlines shuttle on the East Coast of the United States. But you got absolutely nothing when you were a passenger. You paid for your fare in flight, and that was it. All the flight attendants did was collect fares. If you wanted a glass of water, forget it. The whole service was sort of a cattle run. There was no preassignment of seats, so as soon as you boarded the aircraft, people rushed through to grab the seat they wanted, and people fell all over themselves in the process.

Super Shuttle became our showcase. It was the key item we offered in our domestic market, and we had to make it damn good to make sure that people appreciated it and would want to fly BA on other routes. We had four shuttle routes in and out of London (Belfast, Ireland, was added), and they became very busy routes. We were carrying 3 million passengers a year just on those four shuttle routes out of a total of what, at the time, were maybe 17 million passenger journeys a year across all our flights.

After Super Shuttle, the next thing we launched was 'Super Club,' which was enhanced travel for business-class passengers on our intercontinental flights. That was fairly revolutionary at the time, as well. We were the first to provide an enhanced level of service to business-class passengers. Since that time, of course, we've gone on and tried to be quite creative when it comes to seating and comfort factors and different service levels.

So very shortly after assuming the helm at BA, you took concrete steps to create new products, services, and customer perceptions. What about people? What did you do to get them on board with what you were doing?

Marshall: Well, we quickly realized that while we could be quite creative when it came to developing new products and services, we had to do something with the people of the company, as well. Their morale was low and had to be picked up.

One reason morale was low was that the company, prior to my arrival, had been cut back in size enormously. When I arrived, we were down to 41,000 employees from a high of 58,500. Some 17,000 people had left the company in recent years.

When I arrived, I was told we had to cut another 6,000 people. I eventually came to the conclusion that a sensible level for us to bottom out at was 36,500. So we moved about 4,000 more people out of the organization within three to four months of my arrival. At that point, I told employees, 'Look, this is where I believe we can stop our severance programs, and, provided you do a good job and customers respond, we can stabilize at this level and start to create new jobs as our business improves.'

But to get people to work in new ways, we needed a major change in the company's culture. That meant refocusing everyone on the customer, on the marketplace, and away from the exclusively engineering and operations focus we'd had. That had to be done, of course, without sacrificing safety, technical, or maintenance standards. And that proved tricky. People had difficulty understanding why I kept hammering away at the need to focus on customers while also saying, 'We've got to fly these aircraft at a very high technical standard, too.' The focus before had always been on the technical side alone, but I made the point repeatedly that we had to do both. It was at this point that we saw the explicit need for a culture-change program.

What things did you do to change BA's culture?

Marshall: The first thing we did was to launch a program called 'Putting People First,' using outside consultants to formulate the program and deliver it to BA employees. 'Putting People First' was a two-day seminar. We took roughly 150 employees at a time and drew people from various departments within BA and from various geographical areas. The program focused on how one creates better relationships with people, with one's fellow employees, with customers, even with members of one's own family.

When we started delivering this program, I was anxious to inculcate its principles into the minds of front-line people—those who had direct contact with passengers, including people in customer-service jobs, check-in agents, flight attendants, pilots, and reservations agents. But interestingly, about six weeks after the program began, a delegation of four people representing other departments not involved in the program came to me. They told me that I needed to understand that if they didn't do their jobs well and in accordance with the approach espoused in this program, it'd be difficult for the people in the front-line jobs to do *theirs*. They were saying that our new approach had to be a team approach, and they wanted to be part of the team.

What was your reaction when this "delegation" showed up on your doorstep?

Marshall: It was like manna from heaven! It indicated to me that we'd overcome initial cynicism about the program that we'd observed in the first few weeks of offering it. Initially, people had viewed this program as a management gimmick. Nothing more. But clearly, the appearance of this delegation told me that people throughout the company were asking to be involved in change *in a substantive way*.

From then on, we mixed all kinds of BA employees in the sessions of 'Putting People First' we delivered. We had people from back-office departments mixed in with individuals from front-line departments. Nobody was allowed to wear a uniform. Everyone wore a name tag, but only with first names on them.

One thing that made these programs very successful, I believe, is the fact that I, as Chief Executive, always spoke at the end of each session. I personally closed some 40 percent of all the 'Putting People First' programs that we ran over two-and-a-half years. I'd speak to people for about 20 minutes, tell attendees what our objectives were, what our vision of the company for the future was, and what we expected of them as part of that. After that, I'd answer questions and spend an additional hour or so having tea or coffee with people. That gave me the chance to talk to a lot of people individually and to hear people's concerns and enthusiasm.

For this part of the program, we'd also have 10 or 15 other senior managers in attendance, as well. Managers had to mix with employees, listen to their views, and hear their ideas about how to make BA better.

Did having managers mix with employees this way represent a big culture change at BA?

Marshall: Indeed! Up to this time, managers at BA had always been referred to as 'balcony' managers. Use of that term stemmed from the fact that, in the principal terminal at Heathrow Airport at that time, Terminal 1, there was a balcony running around above the main concourse where all the check-in positions were. Most managers and supervisors were located on the balcony level, and employees used to say that managers would come out, look over the balcony, and go back into their offices. They wouldn't come down and spend time with check-in agents. In other words, they wouldn't practice management by walking around.

As part of 'Putting People First,' we concentrated very heavily on getting managers more involved with employees and, as a consequence, with customers, as well. I didn't expect managers to actually perform check-in functions, but just having them there, in the presence of check-in personnel more, began to make a real difference. It made managers seem much more accessible.

Was the reaction to this program consistently enthusiastic?

Marshall: Yes, very much so. It took us about two-and-a-half years to put all our employees worldwide through the 'Putting People First' program. Then it became obvious we couldn't leave it at that. So we put another program in place, largely in response to employee suggestions, called 'A Day in the Life.' This was a training program that acquainted employees with how everything inside the company came together to ensure that aircraft departed on time and that we made a profit. The program consisted of 'snapshots' into the daily workings of nine key departments. We had people from these departments put on 45-minute presentations. We took 150 people at a time through this program and divided them up into nine groups, and they went from one module of training to another throughout the course of a day.

Still another program we implemented inside the company was called 'To Be The Best.' This program, which encouraged employees to think about how we could best deal with our competitors, involved people in making simulated business decisions about the business using an interactive computer program. Everyone from pilots and counter personnel to claims agents and baggage handlers took part in the program.

For example, as part of this training program, people were asked whether BA should raise or lower its fares in response to what a competitor did. Based on the decisions people made in these simulations, it would result either in BA being a successful competitor or going bankrupt trying to outguess its competition. This program was a very powerful exercise for everybody involved and a great team-builder. It gave many people inside the company whose paths had never crossed before the chance to work together in problem-solving teams. Pilots for example, had a chance to learn about the challenges baggage handlers faced in getting planes away on time, and vice versa.

These programs formed key elements in your culture-change strategy as it related to employees. Talk about the transformation efforts you targeted at managers.

Marshall: Well, of course, managers went through the 'Putting People First' program just as other employees did. But we realized that we had to address certain management issues in a specific kind of way if we were to drive real culture change inside the company.

For example, we had to build greater trust with employees, foster more teamwork, and get employees to be more participative in decision-making. That's where you, Warner, were involved, helping us to develop the 'Managing People First' program, which was based on the culture-change analysis we conducted using the Burke-Litwin model of change. From that analysis, we determined that changing our management practices was critical to our future success. Doing so would create a critical link between employees and our business goals.

'Managing People First' was a five-day seminar in which we took our managers away for in-depth training. Most of them went to our training college, about an hour's drive from Heathrow, for this program. We ran this program for over five years, delivering it 110 times in that five-year period. We had roughly 25 managers—a mix of senior, middle, junior, and promising supervisory personnel—in each class.

Like the other programs we ran, this program focused on helping managers take an approach to management and supervision that emphasized not just traditional technical requirements of running an airline, but also people management. We knew we had to focus on managing people differently if we wanted to create strong customer loyalty and satisfaction and engender strong employee loyalty and job motivation. Looking back on it, 'Managing People First' was a program we very much needed to help drive a new set of values within BA, values that, as I mentioned before, combined the need for technical and engineering excellence with a strong imperative to provide superlative customer service.

I made a particular point of attending every one of these 'Managing People First' sessions. I spent two to three hours with each group. I talked with people about our goals, our thoughts for the future. I got people's input about what we needed to do to improve our service and operations. The whole thing proved to be a very useful and productive dialogue. We found it so valuable, in fact, that in cases when I was away, we offered people the opportunity to come back and have a follow-up session with me. So I really did talk to all 110 groups in that five-year period.

You were obviously committed to putting your own personal imprint on the company's change efforts.

Marshall: That's absolutely fundamental, especially with culture change. Employees have to see that it isn't just senior executives but also the top executive who is deeply committed to such efforts.

So here it is, 17 years since you joined BA. What have you learned about people—and about yourself as a leader—as you've managed successful change and sustained it in this organization to this day?

Marshall: What I've learned is that, among most people, there is an innate desire to do well and to do well not only for themselves, but also for their employer. In my view, people operate at their best if they're given the right direction and the right leadership.

In that regard, let me say that, when I first came here, BA was a highly unionized company and, in fact, still is. Over time, however, I think it's fair to say that employees, who at one time looked only to the union for direction and leadership, now look at management for direction and leadership. And that, in my mind, is the way it should be. It suggests to me that feelings of loyalty, support—wanting to get on with things and wanting to work for a successful organization—are the things utmost in the minds and hearts of most everyone with BA today.

What advice would you offer to other executives responsible for driving change initiatives in their organizations?

Marshall: First, do things to generate customer loyalty. If you don't have the customer on your side, you can literally forget about everything else. You aren't going to make any money if you don't have customers. And if you don't have any customers, you won't have jobs for employees or relationships with suppliers and providers. And, thus, you won't have anything to offer to the community at large.

Second, recognize that when you embark on change, you're embarking on a very long-term commitment, and, as CEO, you must be willing to accept that commitment. When we initially went into our culture-change program, I did it with the belief that it would take five years. I subsequently discovered that it wasn't anything like five years but probably closer to ten. As we got close to ten, I realized that if you really embark on culture change, a true culture-change program, then you must push that goal for a generation, until you have the majority, a significant majority, of employees who joined the company *after* you embarked on that culture-change program.

You'd argue then that sustaining successful change is a continuous process?

Marshall: Absolutely. For that reason, in fact, we started delivering 'Putting People First' programs again in the spring of 1999. We think the program is absolutely essential to BA retaining its focus on people.

What other advice would you offer executives responsible for leading change efforts?

Marshall: Once you start, don't slow down, or you will find your company slipping in performance and slipping back into old behaviors. People sometimes want to see the past through rose-colored spectacles. Change is a long-term process that will involve a lot of your time, your *personal* time, in making sure that people understand that change is key to your company's success.

Chapter Conclusions

As we can see from this interview with Colin Marshall, he was and remains today a committed change leader. But what's most interesting about him is *how* he has succeeded as a leader.

While poised, knowledgeable, and articulate, one would not describe Marshall as "charismatic." Successful leadership does not equate in every case with charisma. Marshall's success comes from his unequivocal commitment to changing BA, and this commitment manifested itself both in his consistency of effort and his persistence. He meant what he said and acted accordingly.

Note from the interview that Marshall attended many of the "Putting People First" programs and *all* of the "Managing People First" programs over a five-year period. His persistence (and consistency) in preaching the BA vision and mission and in "staying the course" was astounding.

To Change Culture, You Need to Change People's Behavior

A second thing that becomes clear from this interview is that bringing about real culture change at BA—transforming the company from being an "engineering-driven" company into a "market-driven" enterprise—required focusing on the *behaviors* of people, particularly managers. In BA's case, the new behavioral practices that Marshall and Nick Georgiades, BA's head of human resources, worked on instilling in managers included: openness and candor (not previously practiced in BA), trust, teamwork, and participative management styles.

It was by concentrating on these *new* behaviors, measuring those behaviors via performance appraisals, and then rewarding them via a pay-for-performance system that BA was able to begin changing its culture from within. Indeed, the BA transformation story shows that culture change occurs not by focusing on "changing culture" but when you focus on changing people's *behaviors*. When you change behaviors, a shift in attitudes and values occurs. As a result, real and *sustainable* culture change follows.

Manage Others as You Would Yourself Be Managed

One more thing. The BA transformation story points up the critical link that must be forged between employee job performance and organizational performance. This is essential if real changes in culture and customer perceptions are to occur.

Organizational psychologist Ben Schneider of the University of Maryland, who has written extensively on service organizations, notes that the way in which employees are treated by their supervisors has direct consequences for customer satisfaction. During our work with BA, we used this research as the underpinning for many of the change activities we undertook. To transform BA from being an "engineering driven" company into one that was "market-driven," managers became "targets of opportunity." We followed the principle that if BA managers could learn to treat their direct reports in a more caring manner, these front-line employees would, in turn, learn to treat BA's customers in a more caring manner.

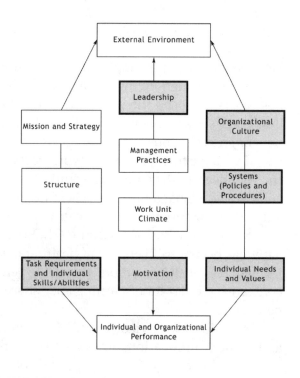

External Environment

Leadership

Mission and Strategy

Organizational
Culture

Management
Practices

Structure

Systems
(Policies and
Procedures)

Work Unit
Climate

Task Requirements
and Individual
Skills/Abilities

Motivation

Individual Needs
and Values

Individual and Organizational
Performance

7 The Learning Leader: How AlliedSignal Uses Learning to Drive Business Transformation

"Yesterday, we measured the success of organizations by their physical assets: factories, employees, inventories. Today it is intellectual capital that determines who wins and who loses in the marketplace. From the very beginning of AlliedSignal's transformation, when every employee received extensive total quality training, we have been committed to building our intellectual capital."

—Larry Bossidy, CEO AlliedSignal

How well does your organization use learning to help drive business transformation, process improvement, and product innovation?

How good is it, for example, at using training and development efforts to inculcate new work values, to align employees with business goals, to speed the pace at which new production methods or best practices are spread throughout the organization, or to support new or emerging business strategies?

To Morristown, NJ-based AlliedSignal, employee learning is at the very heart of the company's ability to compete in today's fiercely competitive global industries of aerospace, engineered materials, and automotive products. And it's a strategy that's clearly working.

Since Larry Bossidy became CEO back in late 1991, the company has been a solid engine of profit and earnings growth, increasing its stock value by more than 700 percent while achieving 29 consecutive quarters of earnings-per-share increases of at least 13 percent.

And Bossidy, a vigorous advocate of business transformation and product innovation, vows that the company will keep achieving annual earnings-per-share growth of 13 percent to 17 percent year after year, while predicting that corporate revenues should reach $18.5 billion by 2000.

Leveraging Learning and Intellectual Capital

Bossidy's approach to growing AlliedSignal's bottom line relies on a four-step approach:

1. Be aggressive about developing new technologies.

2. Transform technologies into new products, and accelerate their commercialization.

3. Expand AlliedSignal operations on a global basis.

4. Make select acquisitions that complement the company's existing businesses.

Wall Street analysts say it's a tall order to fill, given growth constraints in some of AlliedSignal's key markets. Yet Bossidy says he's committed to sustaining the growth that, between 1991 and early 1999, increased the company's market capitalization from $4 billion to more than $30 billion today. The ultimate key to doing it depends on a fifth element: developing people and leveraging learning across AlliedSignal's nine independent businesses.

To stay competitive, Bossidy bets on *people*, not strategy. He realizes that employees need to know how to talk to customers, suppliers, and to each other as part of nurturing the brain trust that drives the research and development of new products. Thus Allied-Signal invests 2 percent of payroll annually on employee development. Company employees are required to have a minimum of 40 hours of company-paid, job-related training each year. Moreover, all employees, including Bossidy, have a training-and-development plan in place to help them continuously expand their base of skills.

Committed to Being a Learning Leader

It's all part of AlliedSignal's effort to be "a learning leader," as company President and Chief Operating Officer Fred Poses puts it. "I've often said that our buildings are no different from our competitors', nor is our machinery fundamentally different. Certainly our dollars are no greener. The thing that has and will continue to differentiate us from our competitors is our people and what they know," he told us in an interview.

But Poses is quick to add that that doesn't mean the company pursues learning for its own sake. "Too many companies check off the boxes and say they've presented training," he says. "Our learning is targeted. I always ask people, 'Are you getting the right learning to do the job?' I'm always seeking feedback on how we can make our learning better."

An Earnings Leader as well as a Learning Leader

While the emphasis on being a "learning leader" has clearly helped AlliedSignal become an *earnings* leader, there have been other payoffs from using learning efforts to drive business goals, one being the amount of in-house bench talent the company has been able to nurture over the last eight years. AlliedSignal employees now fill 65 percent of all job vacancies that come up, compared to just 30 percent that were filled in-house back in 1991, says Donnee Ramelli, AlliedSignal's Vice President of Learning and Organization Development.

In recent years, Bill and several of his PricewaterhouseCoopers colleagues have worked extensively with AlliedSignal's senior leaders in connection with the company's transformation efforts, going back to 1991, when the company first implemented quality in a drive to bring greater speed to its manufacturing processes. Today, that work continues as the company moves forward to implement Six Sigma™ methods and approaches throughout the entire corporation. An ambitious "next generation" approach to quality improvement that involves painstaking analysis and determination of customer requirements, Six Sigma's goal is to produce products that are nearly defect-free. This goal is accomplished through a rigorous process of aligning a company's business processes (e.g., R&D, manufacturing, etc.) with those of its customers, in order to fill customer needs and product specifications exactly. Implementing Six Sigma successfully in any organization requires intense organizational focus, supported by dogged, even single-minded attention to training.

We sat down with Ramelli in AlliedSignal's Learning Center in Morristown to talk with him about the ways, both strategic and tactical, that AlliedSignal uses learning initiatives of different kinds to drive business growth, process improvement, and sustained marketplace competitiveness. We talked also about how individual, project, and team-based learning have become key links in tying business strategy to employee behaviors and how that is helping AlliedSignal move forward toward achieving all its business goals.

Donnee, talk about your role as AlliedSignal's Chief Learning Officer. That's still something of a unique job to hold in a company today.

Ramelli: We have nine businesses in our corporation, nine strategic business units, and they're all trying to be the leader in their industries. My role, as corporate learning officer, is to help develop and implement learning strategies that will make that happen.

AlliedSignal seems more intentional than many companies when it comes to using learning to drive continuous change. You've obviously determined that this is critical to your competitiveness. Describe how the company's emphasis on using learning and training to drive change came about.

™Six Sigma is a federally registered trademark and servicemark of Motorola, Inc.

Ramelli: When Larry came on board and the leadership of the company began to embrace a new set of values (Customers, Integrity, People, Teamwork, Speed, Innovation, and Performance), we realized that we could bring about a powerful change in how we performed if we made sure people really understood the vision and values of the organization and made a commitment to new ways of working. So in 1991 and '92, we embarked on getting people to apply total quality principles, tools, and techniques to the work they were doing, both in teams and as individuals.

We also developed a 'learning framework' that is the basis for all the employee development we do here at AlliedSignal today. Training and development opportunities are all organized under the banner of different 'success attributes,' each of which we feel is critical to supporting the company's business values. There are ten of these attributes, and they include such things as: Customer Focus, Vision and Purpose, Bias for Action, Values and Ethics, People Development, Performance, Teamwork, Innovation, and Business Acumen.

It sounds as if development of these success attributes helped sharpen the focus and purpose of training efforts here. Didn't it also lead to a fundamental philosophical shift about how training should be conducted?

Ramelli: Yes. In the early 1990s, when we first started talking about linking employee learning to business results, we were talking mostly about giving people 'traditional training,' where somebody is teaching content and others are there to learn. Today, learning is much more 'action oriented.' We see learning as being about people exploring business problems together and coming up with solutions to problems.

Talk more about that.

Ramelli: Well, for example, when it comes to understanding our customers' needs, we need to be able to listen to customers, ask them questions, interact with them and with suppliers as well. Doing those things requires strong 'customer engagement' skills. At the same time, here inside the company, we need to be able to share information, key learnings, and other insights with one another as part of developing new technologies and new products. The skills required to do these things—open communication and collaboration, for example—don't come from being in classrooms, and they don't come from books or hypothetical exercises. They come only from working with one another in the workplace and with customers and suppliers in situations where people are doing *real* things and working on *real* problems.

Can you give us an example of action learning as you practice it here at AlliedSignal today?

Ramelli: Yes. In both our total quality and Six Sigma efforts, we use action learning extensively. In our Six Sigma programs, for example, we have employees work on real business problems and projects. Often they do this in teams with customers, which is ideal, since we're using Six Sigma to align our own business processes with those of our customers. Thus far, over 50 client companies of ours have been involved in these collaborative learning opportunities with AlliedSignal, out of which have come real solutions, not only to customers' problems but also to our own. In 1998, we realized about $500 million in savings based on Six Sigma projects that we had teams of AlliedSignal employees and customers work on together. We estimate there's as much as $1.5 billion more in savings and efficiencies we can realize by collaborating more with one another internally and with customers. In 1999, for example, we expect to generate another $600 million in savings through Six Sigma.

It seems that integrating learning and real work this way has helped AlliedSignal cement relationships with customers, cut costs, improve business productivity, and boost product quality.

Ramelli: Absolutely.

You also use learning and development initiatives to support innovation goals, to reduce R&D times, and to support aggressive business growth objectives. How does AlliedSignal accomplish all that through training and development of employees?

Ramelli: One of the core premises of all our training here is that we, as a company and as individuals, are in business to create value, to expand the markets we're already in, and, in some cases, to 'go to other ponds,' as somebody here put it the other day, by which they meant go into entirely new markets. Our learning and training efforts, therefore, are focused on these things. Take innovation, for example. Larry often says that innovation is the very key to our business success, and it's true. Currently, we have over 1,500 growth projects in various stages of development throughout the company. These projects all focus around the research and development of what we call 'killer technologies' that will be the basis of new products and that we're planning to apply in various ways across all the businesses we're in. These projects will be key to us keeping our competitive edge. In fact, the top 50 of these projects will account for $4.5 billion in sales over the next three years. The key to completing them successfully is to have people who can do the tough work required to problem-solve, to innovate, and to develop new products from these new technologies. Action-learning opportunities give employees the chance to do *all* these things.

What are some of these 'killer' technologies?

Ramelli: Many of the technologies now in development relate to how materials work together or the way that we can make products more dependable or more efficient in our customers' operations. Others will become the basis for future generations of existing products, for new and improved ground proximity warning systems, turbochargers, turbogenerators, and environmentally friendly refrigerants to replace CFCs.

Each of the new technologies we're developing or enhancing today got selected after we looked around, talked to customers, and looked at both the markets we were in and the ones we wanted to be in. We determined that, if we focused on these areas in particular, applied the right resources, research, energy, and thinking to developing products based on these technologies, we could make a huge difference in the markets where we operate. But, again, the ability to develop these technologies and to innovate around the right things means employees have to have good customer-engagement skills. That's really the key to all this. They need to have good relationships with customers, understand customers' needs, and be able to develop world-class products as an outflow of that.

To develop new 'killer technologies' means you need employees who possess both 'soft' skills—such as the ability to communicate and collaborate with others—but also 'hard' (technical) skills required to do intense R&D work. You have a very robust employee-development process in place here at AlliedSignal. You require every employee to have at least 40 hours of needs-based training a year. How is AlliedSignal's employee-development process designed to reinforce specific job requirements as well as company values and strategic business goals?

Ramelli: Well, the real employee-development process for us starts not in training but in performance management and development discussions that employees have with their supervisors at least twice a year. As part of these feedback and development discussions, it's our goal to have employees understand and own what they need to do to develop to their full potential. Employees need to own their development plans. Supervisors and managers also own part of the responsibility, but it's mostly with the employee.

One thing we encourage managers to do as part of performance appraisals is to deliver feedback that's candid and concrete. Recently, I attended a meeting where I heard one business executive say that to not give candid feedback to an employee, a talented employee, is to cheat that individual out of their future. If you give people concrete feedback in a constructive way, they'll figure out how to get better, and when they do, our products and services will be better and so will our bottom-line.

Another thing we do is to use learning and training opportunities to reinforce behaviors that mirror our business values. So, as we've discussed, we use the 'success attributes'—things like 'customer focus,' 'teamwork,' 'leadership,' and 'innovation'—as the conceptual framework for helping people develop key leadership competencies.

Let's say I received feedback that my customer-focus skills weren't what they needed to be. I could take some in-house courses to help me improve those skills. I could seek out others in the company as mentors and coaches to help me develop better customer-focus skills. There might also be an outside course I could take or an internal project I could become part of that would help me grow these necessary skills. We want to encourage and support all these individual growth alternatives because, at the end of the day, they help us and our bottom-line.

What kinds of things does AlliedSignal do, on an ongoing basis, to make sure that people continue to grow professionally?

Ramelli: One thing we do as part of our people-development process is help people look at what may be challenging next work assignments. We're always asking questions like: 'How can we stretch people?' 'How can we help employees expand their knowledge of our business?' 'How can we make them more customer focused?' 'What skills does that person need to develop next if they're to move to the next level with their career? Is it by putting people on cross-functional projects, by charging people with leading a change initiative, or by doing something else?'

All of the changes we've made here at AlliedSignal in recent years, both to processes and to our organizational structure, have been housed in a kind of action-learning or project-focused approach that's intended to help people continue to grow and develop. We've created literally thousands of opportunities for people to guide or lead or participate or contribute in different projects and different initiatives. We've worked hard to give people assignments that are clearly stretches for them because that's where real learning occurs.

As part of applying your 'learning framework,' you assess the stage at which an employee is in his or her career. You then use that as the basis for tailored employee development. It sounds very logical, but outline the rationale for doing it.

Ramelli: We think it's good to identify the stage of development at which an employee may be within his or her career because it provides a good baseline for planning employee-development efforts. It also helps drive closer alignment of a person's skills with the existing or emerging needs of the business.

We think basically in terms of three stages: People who are at Stage One are what we refer to as 'individual contributors to the organization.' They work either as individuals or as members of a team. People at Stage Two are in a position to lead and manage others. This group can include anybody from first-time supervisors to experienced managers. People at this stage of development are, in our view, able to lead significant initiatives inside the company, key projects, and so on. People at Stage Three are what we view as 'strategic leaders.' This includes people at the general manager level as well as senior-level functional leaders who have strategic responsibilities. Individuals in this category are those who lead strategic processes and initiatives but who don't have individuals reporting directly to them. These are the three stages that we typically see any employee progressing through during the course of their career, and we use this staged approach to help people define and delineate learning and development paths that are appropriate to them.

Regardless of what stage a person may be at in their career, however, the emphasis is always on hands-on learning, right? You want learning experiences to be grounded in the context of solving practical business problems.

Ramelli: Absolutely, and here's why: 70 percent of how people learn as adults comes from challenging work assignments, where people have to work hard to figure out new ways to be successful. Twenty percent comes from working with others—role models, coaches, peers, and so forth. Even people who aren't that helpful can teach us to be better in the roles we play. Finally, 10 percent of learning, in our estimation, comes from training courses and workshops. The whole development thrust here at AlliedSignal is on that first 90 percent. That's not to say we don't send people to classrooms. But when we do, we try to use action-learning projects to ensure that we apply learning to real-world situations and derive real results from having people work together on problems.

Is that how a company like AlliedSignal builds employee commitment to change and continuous organizational renewal? By getting people energized to solve problems?

Ramelli: Definitely. Giving people the opportunity to develop on the job—even as they are *doing* their job—leads to good employee retention. It leads to people who are loyal and committed, who 'own the business,' and who do so with passion. And at the end of the day, that's what we want: 70,000 people who are doing that.

Most people, when they think of a manufacturing company, imagine a pretty tough, macho culture. They don't picture a place where there's a lot of learning and sharing going on. What kinds of organizational structures have you put in place to create a collaborative work culture here—to support the values of cross-functional communication, collaboration, and the 'boundaryless organization' that Jack Welch of GE, among others, has become such a big proponent of?

Ramelli: In all parts of AlliedSignal today, we have opportunities and mechanisms for information-sharing among people. We have different types of forums, conferences, and workshops to deal not just with manufacturing issues but also with human-resources issues, financial processes, and the supply chain. We also use the company's intranet to link our efforts. Establishing these 'forums,' if you will, has become a corporate-wide practice that has led to the widespread sharing of product- and process-improvement ideas and to the sharing of new know-how, techniques, and individual insights among people.

We talked a few minutes ago about how you're using Six Sigma methods and approaches to drive changes in work processes and improve efficiencies. Until recently, your Six Sigma efforts were limited to one part of the organization. Now you're using training and learning channels to introduce Six Sigma principles and business practices throughout all of AlliedSignal. What's driving that at this point in time?

Ramelli: Well, it's interesting. We've used Six Sigma practices for some time now in our manufacturing operations, and we've improved our efficiency and productivity enormously.

Well, as a matter of fact, wasn't it through using Six Sigma methods and approaches that AlliedSignal found a way to recycle old carpet and thus avoid the need to build a new carpet-fiber processing plant?

Ramelli: Yes. Because of Six Sigma methods, we found a way to recycle old carpet, thus negating the need for us to build a new $85 million dollar plant. The new recycling process now in place is going to save us between $30 million and $40 million a year. Those savings emerged because our people were able to apply critical thinking approaches to an existing work process and redesign it to achieve much higher levels of efficiency.

So far, we've trained thousands of our employees from every business unit and from every level in advanced Six Sigma manufacturing techniques. Trainees have learned how to analyze manufacturing processes in factories. They've determined where the highest levels of defects were occurring and addressed the problems, either by fixing them or eliminating processes in some cases.

Now we want to bring Six Sigma to all other parts of the organization because we see it as the way to bring quality and speed to still other business areas and, as a consequence, provide more value to our supply chain.

But implementing Six Sigma isn't easy—even though training and development provide great vehicles for spreading it throughout an organization.

Ramelli: No, there are always challenges. Six Sigma involves the use of a lot of advanced quantitative and statistical methods and applying those to work processes to reduce error rates. Not only does it require a lot of leadership commitment to implement, but it also requires a lot of training to fully understand and apply on an everyday basis. But if you can do it successfully and really reduce error rates to a mere three per million, it puts your company in a league practically by itself. And that's what we're aiming to do.

How does Six Sigma fit into the company's ongoing transformation efforts?

Ramelli: Six Sigma represents the 'third generation' of quality improvement efforts here at AlliedSignal. As I said earlier, back in the early 1990s we introduced total quality concepts and principles, such as team-based work. When we saw how effective they were in helping us align people with our emerging business values, we moved on to introduce additional quality tools such as advanced statistical tools for measuring performance and for listening to and understanding the needs of customers.

Now, we're striving to reach the next organizational productivity 'plateau.' To get there, we need to implement Six Sigma organization-wide, and the Six Sigma training we're now doing is providing the 'delivery channel' for getting this knowledge further out into our organization.

It sounds as if doing so will create an even stronger alignment of people and processes to support business goals. What strategic and tactical goals does AlliedSignal want to achieve through use of Six Sigma organization-wide, and how are learning efforts designed to help you achieve those goals?

Ramelli: At a *strategic* level, our goal with Six Sigma is to align all our employees—their behaviors and skills—with core business processes across *all* AlliedSignal businesses. On an organization-wide level, that means making sure that learning programs and activities focus on helping employees understand not only our customers but also the markets in which we operate. We're using these efforts to support the push for greater innovation, as well, of course.

When we talk about applying Six Sigma at the *workplace* or *job* level, our goal there is to help employees learn how to engage with customers more effectively. We also want them to be able to measure their own work performance (and our performance as a company) against customer requirements. We want people to be able to ask themselves questions such as, 'Are we really filling the bill?' 'Are we giving customers what they need?' 'Are we giving it to them defect-free, on-time, or even ahead of time?' 'Are we thinking of new ways to create customer value?' It's questions like those we want employees to be able to answer.

So teaching people Six Sigma approaches will enable them to engage with customers in new and more effective ways, ways that will differentiate AlliedSignal from its competitors?
Ramelli: Exactly.

From our conversation, it would seem that learning programs, objectives, and activities here are well-positioned—both strategically and organizationally—to support AlliedSignal's growth, innovation, and customer goals. What, in your mind, remains to be done?
Ramelli: For starters, we need to complete the quality journey we're on. We need to get every one of our business processes up to Six Sigma standards. Our learning efforts are critical to doing that because they emphasize a 'partnership approach' to solving problems. Sometimes that partnership approach involves teams of AlliedSignal employees working closely together. In other cases, it involves company–customer teams joining hands and minds to solve problems. So, that's one thing.

Second, we need to become even more of an 'outside–in' company than we are today. We need to understand *instinctively* what customers want. How, for example, can we use Six Sigma to keep improving the quality of products we offer to customers? How can we use Six Sigma methods and approaches to drive us toward even fewer product defects than we experience today? We've taken a lot of time and gone to extraordinary effort to build the skills, the talent, and the potential inside this organization to be a world-class company, yet the battle continues. We've done a good job, but, as Larry often says, we need to go to the next level.

What does that mean?

Ramelli: It means that the challenge for us now is to get out of our comfort zone of experience and go be with customers more. We need to travel down the value chain to end-users, to consumers, so that we can understand better what differentiates our products from those of our competitors. If we forced ourselves to spend more time with customers than we do now, if we walked in their shoes for a while, we'd understand their competitive pressures and their economics better than we do today. I think we'd find ourselves in situations, too, where we could tell somebody, 'Hey, we know how to make that molecule lighter' or 'We know how to make that part extrudable.' I'm not suggesting, necessarily, that our salespeople spend more time with customers, but perhaps some of our folks from our technology areas, from engineering and manufacturing, could.

Doesn't that happen now? You've talked about the fact that one of the keys to AlliedSignal's success is that you talk to customers.

Ramelli: We do, but the kinds of additional discoveries I'm talking about here don't occur in-house, even if you've got great team collaboration and you invite customers in. You have to travel out to be with customers where they work and live, and I'd argue it's important to travel as far downstream as you can. We need to make more of an organizational habit of doing that. If we did, we'd find markets for our products we haven't even imagined yet.

Chapter Conclusions

As this chapter shows, AlliedSignal is using learning and employee-development activities (especially action learning) as critical change drivers to help it continue on the quality journey, to foster ever more intimate customer relationships, and to help the company achieve its aggressive growth goals. The company's learning function is very much linked with overarching business goals and organizational values and is viewed by the company's top leaders as a key vehicle both for communicating work expectations and re-inforcing a high-performance culture.

AlliedSignal has moved away from the traditional notion of employee training as a staff function to a far more strategic view of employee development as key to the future vitality and profitabil-ity of the business. Through use of its "learning framework," the company uses employee development as a vehicle for building leadership and technical competencies in employees, which in its view are more essential to business success than either pure tech-nology or business strategy. Learning and training initiatives are also designed to build strong customer-engagement skills and to help employees understand even so basic (but critical) a premise as what kinds of questions to ask their customers on a regular basis. But there's more.

The Marriage of Work and Learning

Ramelli talks with passion about where he sees the integration of work and learning at AlliedSignal going in the future. "To us, the marriage of work and learning is a natural," he says. Indeed, Allied-Signal sees this approach as being of paramount importance in creating strategic marketplace advantage in the increasingly com-petitive aerospace and auto parts marketplace. "We need both these things playing off one another for us to develop the synergy that will help us be competitive on a going-forward basis."

To that end, Ramelli says the next frontier for AlliedSignal is to leverage Web technology to facilitate even faster learning; refine and share business best practices throughout the organization more easily; and create interactive online communities of AlliedSignal employees, customers, and suppliers. "The Internet holds the po-tential for us to learn and work with one another across time and space and to realize benefits that simply aren't possible using tra-ditional work-and-training approaches," he says. "We're already taking significant steps with Web-based learning approaches be-cause they will enable us to address the issues of speed and tech-nology advances in the future in ways we can't do currently. In essence, the blending of technology and training will create un-beatable opportunities for new learning and for the acceleration of change here at AlliedSignal on a continuous basis."

So how might you use training, learning initiatives, and employee development as change drivers in *your* organization? First you need to ask yourself:

- **Is my company's top leadership actively engaged in linking learning to change goals?** Is it highly involved in spearheading the importance of learning initiatives in my organization? At AlliedSignal, all nine heads of AlliedSignal businesses are regularly involved in launching new learning initiatives, as are Larry Bossidy and Fred Poses.

- **Does the culture of my company view learning as an opportunity to improve the business and the individual?** Is it naturally built into the way people in the organization work and learn together?

- **Does the training/learning function in my organization play a strategic role in business goal development, or is its role largely reactive and implementation-oriented once high-level business decisions have been made?**

Developing a Strong Learning Capability Will Be Critical to Managing Successful Change in the Future

Building a high-performance learning function will become increasingly essential to the health and welfare of *all* companies in the years ahead as the pace of change continues to accelerate. In industries as diverse as health care, aerospace, chemicals, pharmaceuticals, and high-tech, the leveraging of intellectual capital to sustain business advantage has never been more critical than it is today.

So how does your own organization stack up? To what extent are you using learning as a change driver in *your* organization today? To what extent is *your* company committed to being a "learning leader?"

If you have effectively and strategically aligned employee development and learning initiatives with large-gauge business goals and strategies, it means you have harnessed a powerful change driver—at a transactional level in your organization—to help drive change efforts forward. If such work still lies before you, it means that you have not yet put in place a fundamental support strut in sustaining your company's change efforts for the long term.

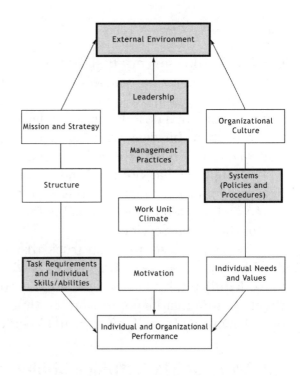

8 Delivering the Future:
The Changing Face of Today's
Postal Service

*"I am one of those who believe that leadership is more important
than ever in organizational life. I think the macho leaders of the past,
with their command-and-control mentality, are uniquely unquali-
fied to lead the organization of the future. The leaders who succeed
in intelligent organizations will be the antithesis of the authoritarian
leaders of our bureaucratic past. Instead of ordering, they will orchestrate. Instead of paying 'yes men,' they will seek out and reward responsible naysayers. Above all, these new leaders will be people who
can articulate a vision that inspires and empowers everyone."*

—Warren Bennis

Bill Henderson, seventy-first Postmaster General of the United States, is a man who has seen the United States Postal Service (USPS) go through tremendous transitions in the course of his lifetime. The son of a postal clerk, Henderson grew up hearing his father talk about his days working as a member of the now-defunct Railway Mail Service, a branch of the U.S. Post Office Department whose origins go back to the 1860s, shortly after the "Iron Horse" first made its appearance on American rails.

As a kid, Henderson recalls his father's strong pride at working for the Postal Service.

"My father had a pickup truck that was filled with a bed of dirt," he says. That way, on winter days when snowfalls made travel to work difficult, his father could put dirt down on the road for traction to ensure that he got to work on time. "You couldn't just pick up the phone and say, 'I won't be in to work today,'" he says.

An Array of Marketplace Challenges

Nowadays, the challenges Henderson faces as the USPS Postmaster General and Chief Executive Officer go far beyond those of simply snow, wind, rain, or dark of night. He's leading the Postal Service at a time when it's dealing with "weather changes" of a different sort —forces like globalization, growing customer expectations, proliferating competition from United Parcel Service (UPS) and Federal Express (FedEx), and the increasing influence of the Internet—which are rapidly changing the business environment in which the Postal Service operates.

It's a challenging time in the life of the USPS, as the agency shifts from being a labor-intensive government-style monopoly to an organization characterized by partnerships and alliances with private sector high-tech companies and mail-service providers.

Using New Yardsticks to Measure Performance

To prepare for greater competition in the next century, the Postal Service has embarked on its first-ever five-year strategic plan as required under the 1993 Government Performance and Results Act (GPRA). The plan, which covers strategic initiatives and business efforts that the Postal Service will undertake between now and 2002, stipulates the use of several metrics to evaluate business performance and organizational effectiveness including: percentage of on-time deliveries, revenue and market share increases and reductions in labor costs. One of the key goals of the strategic plan calls for the Postal Service to reach and sustain a local overnight First-Class Mail delivery rate of 95 percent by 2002 and to increase the two-to-three-day out-of-town First Class Mail delivery rate to 92 percent by that same date.

The challenges the Postal Service faces in today's business environment are unique and intense. Federal regulations set forth in the Postal Reorganization Act of 1970 prevent the Postal Service from offering products and services with prices and characteristics that compare favorably with competitive offerings. These regulations constrain the Postal Service's ability to respond to rapidly changing market conditions and to control costs.

A Proven Leader and Innovator

Still, Henderson believes the Postal Service is in a good position to "leverage its infrastructure and ubiquity" to marketplace advantage in the century ahead, although it will take considerable organizational transformation to achieve. Henderson is no stranger to the principles of organizational change. Indeed, during his Postal Service career, he has been an innovator and leader of change initiatives. As the senior operating manager for the state of North Carolina in the 1980s, he was the first to commit to serving retail customers in "Five Minutes or Less," which has since become the national standard. In 1992, he moved to postal headquarters as Vice President of Employee Relations. There he introduced 360-degree feedback for executives and oversaw the largest downsizing in postal history.

We sat down with Henderson to talk with him about the external business challenges facing the Postal Service today, to understand how the Postal Service is transforming itself organizationally to meet those challenges.

Bill, describe, if you would, the forces driving change in the Postal Service today.

Henderson: The biggest challenge, not just for us, but for everybody, is adjusting to technology. Technology affects the Postal Service at all levels. On the positive side of the ledger, it creates new gadgets that enable us to move mail more rapidly and more accurately, and to reduce our labor intensity. Insofar as products are concerned, that same technology has enabled us to turn junk mail into advertising mail. It enables mailers to accurately target mail recipients, depending on whether they fly-fish, play golf, or whatever. That capability has created a boom in mail volumes.

On the negative side, technology has supplanted some of our core products. Take, for example, business-to-business correspondence. We've had an absolute drop-off in that in the last eight years because everyone, including us, uses electronic mail. Moreover, it's very likely that, in the future, peoples' bill payments will be largely if not entirely electronic. For us, that's $5 billion in hard money for bill payments and another $10 billion for related products that will go away. The actual adoption curve is unclear. It may be 25 years, but it *will* happen.

So on balance, does the Postal Service come out ahead or behind, given advances in technology today?
Henderson: Well, this isn't a doomsday story because, as I just said, even though business-to-business mail has declined, we've had this boom in advertising mail. Moreover, technology will eventually help us manage the mail delivery process more effectively, which will improve our ability to keep pricing in check.

Still, is it fair to say that the Postal Service's revenue streams are shifting?
Henderson: Yes.

So what's the Postal Service doing to develop new technologies that will someday replace more traditional forms of mail delivery yet assure continued profits?
Henderson: Well, for one thing, we're being romanced by the private sector right now to provide an electronic information platform upon which bill payments would travel. In a sense, you could say we're being asked to eat our young because we're being offered a piece of the action if we take part in this arrangement.

A number of big mailers—one of them mails over 100 million letters a month—want us to become involved with them in providing this electronic platform. They fear that if we don't get involved, one of two alternative 'models of the marketplace' will emerge, neither of which they think is good for them.

The first of these is a kind of 'Microsoft economic monopoly model' of the marketplace. In this scenario, a single big company would emerge to own this platform and, in 15 years or so, might feel itself to be in a position to charge tariffs on this platform, on this mail delivery highway, and they don't want that.

The second scenario that could arise, they feel, is a kind of 'cellular-phone industry model' of competition, wherein everybody who is competing has to build their own distribution highway for electronic mail. They don't like that, either, because it's expensive to build, and it suboptimizes market penetration.

So these mailers are looking for a trusted third party that's regulated to become involved with them. They're saying to us, 'Look, you build this electronic highway, and we'll be your customer. We know you can't gouge us on pricing because you're regulated. You're not just sitting there, independent.'

Where do these discussions stand right now?

Henderson: We're in the talking stages with a number of these high-tech companies and exploring what potential partnerships might look like. But I think, potentially, that the future Postal Service will be very much a Jacob's quilt of public and private entities, not simply a government operation. Today, for example, all ten of our Priority Mail processing plants on the East Coast are run by the private sector, and without us they don't exist. We're their only customer, and we'll likely build at least 20 more of these centers around the United States, all of them private sector. So the Postal Service, in 10 or 15 years, will be a combination of private sector and government doing mail service and delivery.

Interesting. Most people probably aren't aware of that. People still view the Postal Service as this monolithic government agency, but, in fact, you're doing what private sector companies do already. You're moving in the direction of strategic alliances, partnerships.

Henderson: Exactly. We even partner with our competitors. For example, we just signed an alliance agreement with 270 Mail Boxes, Etc., outlets to make them post offices. At a policy level, we're also working hard to bring about the deregulation of the Postal Service so that in 10 or 15 years' time, we could very likely look quite different from what we are today.

With all that as context, let's drill down to talk about the people issues you're grappling with today. What are you doing—internally—

to transform how you operate, given all the changes in the external environment that we've been talking about?

Henderson: Well, the biggest challenge internally for us is to create environments in which people can maximize their talents. We don't do that today. In some plants, for example, we have people doing jobs that are the equivalent of putting lugs on wheels, so there's frustration. The way to deal with that is to take the monotonous jobs and have technology do them. We also need to channel people into the more interesting, technical jobs like our maintenance jobs. But doing that takes time, resources, training, and communications, and we still have lots of work to do in those areas. For example, we need to tap the best thinking of our people, and, in many cases, we're not doing that as well as we must.

Can you explain that in more detail?

Henderson: Well, in a bureaucracy the size of ours, one of the real measures of how well you're doing is how well you take people's ideas and suggestions for improving things and actually implement them. If you don't tap into employees' ideas and creativity to solve problems, you won't move forward very fast to bring about change. So one way to know whether you're managing change effectively is to look at the degree to which change is being driven in local facilities by people who work there.

How is the Postal Service doing with that?

Henderson: It varies by location. In my view, though, we're at the very beginning of a critical change process. It's very tough to communicate with 850,000 people and to introduce new metrics or strategic initiatives as called for in the strategic five-year plan. The message gets garbled. Government employees have a lot of potential voices to listen to, not just those of us in senior management at the Postal Service. There are unions, associations, newspapers, the public, the Congress, the President, the media. To the average employee, it sometimes sounds like an orchestra warming up. It's hard to hear any clear message in the din. So people get confused or feel they're getting *mixed* messages about what they're supposed to be doing.

Our job in postal management is to make sense out of all these sounds and to bring some harmony to the change process, to state the vision of where the Postal Service needs to be going in the twenty-first century and how we see ourselves getting there. We're making headway, but we need to make more.

How would you describe the organizational culture here in the Postal Service, both yesterday and today?

Henderson: Prior to 1971, when we didn't have a budget and we had to ask for money from congress, the Postal Service was very service-oriented. Employees considered it an exceptional place to work. It was also very internally focused. That's pretty common with traditional economic monopolies as well as legislative monopolies, as we were then.

Today, in the wake of postal service reform, we're much more outwardly focused—more customer-focused—because our customers are extremely sensitive and we've got a bottom line to generate. In the early years just after postal service reform, we focused on cost-cutting and budgets. Now we're focusing on things like quality and marketing. We have to because there's no guaranteed market share anymore.

Indeed.

Henderson: You know, United Parcel Service was in a situation similar to us for many years. We had a legislative monopoly, and they had an economic monopoly (for rapid mail and freight delivery). I was kidding Jim Kelly, CEO of UPS, about this not too long ago. I said to Jim, 'You know, we didn't have marketing until 1986.' And he said to me, 'Well, we didn't have it until 1985!'

But today it's a new world. Everybody in the mail and freight business has competition. Customers are demanding new and different things, and we've learned to pay attention to them. Nowadays, there isn't a product we offer that isn't in competition against something that somebody else offers. So for at least the last five years, we've been making very focused efforts to get more in front of our customers. That's actually helping now to bind our employees together. We've eased the labor–management tensions somewhat because everybody realizes that the real opponent is the competitor outside our doors.

You said a moment ago that, in an organization this size, communication gets garbled. As you move forward with change, what 'levers' are you pulling internally to achieve it? Obviously, you, as the senior leader, are driving change downward in the organization. What else is going on to communicate new business realities and operating imperatives?

Henderson: Well, we have a new incentive pay system that is moving us in the direction of changing peoples' behaviors. But the most important thing we do today is bring customers in all the time and talk with them. In the city of Chicago, where, in the past, we've had problems, every post office station now has a customer council. The station people don't do anything without talking to the customer council.

Every big city in the United States has a Postal Customer Council. When we link them together at our annual Postal Forums, we have as many as 30,000 customers, suppliers, and postal employees all talking to one another. We link them together face to face and by satellite. Believe me, there's nothing like a live customer with demands and business to offer you to make you change your organization. For years, we didn't talk to customers very much, but that has changed, both at the retail level and at the business level. Recently, for example, we won all of Nordstrom's business, and, as part of the business arrangement we've put in place with them, we are committed to remaining very attuned to their expectations.

Are Postal Councils a new thing?

Henderson: No, but in the past, we didn't use them as effectively as we have in recent years.

Are they like focus groups?

Henderson: No, they're made up of the major customers in different localities. They come to talk about their businesses, and we have business network centers and business service centers to listen to what they're saying. We also have 200 national accounts that we call every five days for one-on-one discussions, to make sure their business is being taken care of. We do this all over the U.S.

So this is all part of an effort to become a more customer-focused organization?

Henderson: Absolutely. We want to grow bigger ears!

Let's switch gears to talk about the new marketing landscape you're facing internationally. How are customer councils and other devices used to keep abreast of customer needs in the international environment?

Henderson: Internationally, we're very active. We're unregulated in the international environment, so we operate more like a business than we do domestically. We don't have pricing controls, for example, as we do domestically, so we're free to price as we want.

The international postal environment today is very competitive. Most people don't realize that Royal Mail (United Kingdom), the German Post, and the Dutch Post are all in the U.S., taking mail from the U.S. as freight, shipping it to Amsterdam or London, converting it to Dutch or Royal mail pieces, then distributing it around Europe. International posts are breaking out of their cocoons, and they're looking at the U.S. much as we look upon Asia today, as a vast, untapped market. It's not direct competition for us yet, but, in the future, when monopoly walls are broken down, it wouldn't surprise me to see the Dutch delivering mail in New York or the Germans delivering it in Chicago. The German Post just bought a billion-dollar logistics company, so they've got marketing aspirations here as they do elsewhere. For their part, the Dutch just invested $20 million in a company here in Washington, D.C., that is a hybrid mail company.

These governments are becoming highly commercialized. They have deep pockets, and they're going to be all over the U.S., so it makes sense for companies like UPS, FedEx, and us to become collectively competitive against these players.

How can the USPS counter-punch, internationally speaking?

Henderson: One way is through strategic alliances. For example, we've put an alliance in place with DHL Worldwide Express to provide two-day business mail delivery to 19 countries in Western Europe. This service is aimed at small and home-based businesses that require reliable service overseas with delivery confirmation, day-certain delivery, and online tracking capabilities. We think it gives our international service a new and very important edge—at very affordable rates.

That's a critical consideration because, globally, the single biggest business driver today is quality. Everybody wants high quality for less money. Just look at the price of clothes nowadays. In so many cases, clothes and other exports are made in countries where the labor cost is cheaper than here. Everything is pushing price-per-unit down, and, with many carriers in the mail delivery game today, quality is skyrocketing. So the only way to survive is to provide higher quality.

If that's so, what's the value-added factor that the U.S. Postal Service brings to the mail delivery equation?

Henderson: First, our infrastructure is already capitalized. Second, of course, the U.S. Postal Service is ubiquitous. We're everywhere. So if we push quality, lower prices for customers will come automatically. That's why our competitors like Federal Express and UPS are so focused on battling the USPS. Look at Priority Mail, for example. It's a high-quality two- to three-day product at a very low price. We're causing price deflation in the marketplace because of our performance in delivering it. Our competitors don't like that because they want to have the premium price for the quality. They were able to get the premium price for the quality until our quality rose to a level of competitiveness. Now market share is coming toward us.

So, the answer is that your economies of scale are kicking in and the fact that you are everywhere?

Henderson: Right. We have a big advantage in that we can leverage our infrastructure.

Do you have new products in the pipeline to make the Postal Service even more competitive?

Henderson: Yes. Our newest product is Parcel Select, which we introduced in early 1999. This service provides deep discounts to businesses to drop parcels at centrally located postal service distribution centers. This service is aimed at high-volume residential shippers, like mail-order and catalogue companies that ship more than 50 boxes per day. It's part of our effort to reclaim the ground-parcel market, and we expect the service to bring in over $1 billion in revenue in fiscal 1999. It's a very attractive service to us because it leverages the fixed costs of local daily delivery.

Bill, in recent years, the U.S. Postal Service has, in fact, achieved significant revenue growth and been able to sustain it. In 1998, you had your fourth straight year with a billion-dollar net profit. What kinds of things has the Postal Service done in the areas of people, systems, and processes to achieve these results?

Henderson: More than anything, we've worked hard to create focus. Let me give you an example. We went to our customers and said to them, 'If you could have anything from us on a consistent basis, what's the one thing you'd most like to have?' They came back consistently saying, 'We'd like overnight mail *overnight.* We understand the two-day and three-day services you offer. They're fine. But more than anything else, we want our overnight mail delivered *overnight.*'

What did you do with that customer input?

Henderson: Back in 1994, we put a new outside metric in place, brought the entire Postal Service management team together in a single room—1,100 top managers—and said to them, 'Does anybody here not believe that overnight service ought to be overnight? I mean, we've been saying this for years, but it isn't overnight! Don't you think it would be a giant step in a positive direction to do this?' And everybody in the room rallied. They said, 'Absolutely!'

At the time, we had scores that showed our performance was awful when it came to overnight mail delivery. We had scores showing that only 40 percent of overnight mail arrived overnight in New York. In Chicago, it was 50 percent. In some places around the country, it was 30 percent!

But over five years, we wrapped a bonus system around improving our scores in overnight mail delivery and made adherence to the scores a very simple, straightforward priority. We said, 'If you don't deliver overnight service overnight, you don't get bonuses, you don't belong in management, and you don't keep your job.'

As part of undertaking that project, we highlighted as many success stories as we could find. For example, when Miami, Florida, hit 90 percent in its overnight delivery rate, we highlighted it. That began to change the attitude of the major metropolitan areas, which until that time had said things like, 'Well, we're never going to do it in New York. They may be able to do it in Harrisburg or Erie, but not in New York.'

By highlighting success stories, though, it began to turn peoples' attitudes around. More than anything else, it began to build confidence in people that they, too, could achieve what we were striving for.

Now, five years later, we've built a very confident management team that feels it can leap tall buildings in a single bound and travel at the speed of light. And over time, the major metropolitan areas have become the blocking backs, the strength in the campaign, which, when you consider where the Chicagos and New Yorks were, is really surprising.

Can you explain that?

Henderson: Well, now New York, for example, is in the high 90s with its overnight delivery rate. We've created 'clubs' inside the Postal Service to celebrate different metros' success rates with overnight delivery. These groups of postal employees have common business goals and objectives. And, in many cases, we've involved peoples' families in the clubs and had different kinds of recognition campaigns.

For example, we have 'Champion Clubs.' These clubs are formed to celebrate a metropolitan area getting what we call a '95–95' rating. That means they've achieved a 95 percent overnight completion rate and a 95 percent customer satisfaction rate. If you achieve both of those things at the same time, we consider you a real winner. You've achieved both the perception of customer service and the reality of superlative performance.

Recently, people in the field created another club called 'Groundbreakers.' A metropolitan postal area becomes a 'Groundbreaker' when it achieves a 96–96 rating on performance and customer satisfaction. I didn't create the Groundbreakers concept; it came straight from the field. But it shows the amount of enthusiasm that has sprouted up over the years about the Postal Service's ability to perform at very high levels.

People throughout the Postal Service have really become believers in their ability to perform.

Henderson: Exactly, and that's the key. I distinctly remember making a speech to postal executives and managers five years ago about how nice it would be if we could guarantee that nine out of ten letters in America that are mailed overnight actually got there overnight. People came up to me and said, 'Bill, you don't really think that's possible, do you? Not for thirty-two cents.'

Now it's five years later, and we've had 16 quarters of solid performance improvement around overnight delivery. Every quarter we've broken the prior records. It's the result of people having confidence in their ability to perform.

You obviously empowered people with your challenge, but it sounds like you also made it clear that people had to perform. You put their feet to the fire.

Henderson: I simply made them believe that they shouldn't be in management unless they could perform. I didn't threaten them. I just said, 'You know, if you can't practice medicine, you're not a doctor.'

Since that time, have you used that same call to arms to raise other performance metrics?

Henderson: Yes. We did it on revenues. We said, 'Wouldn't it be nice to make a billion dollars.' So we used the same approach, and guess what? We made a billion-two. And then postal employees made a billion-six.

How did you do it?

Henderson: You know, if you win the hearts of people, they'll find the tools to succeed. I mean, they'll want to go to process management training, they'll learn new performance techniques, and they'll want 360-degree feedback—if you present it to them as a challenge. If, on the other hand, you shove those things down their throats, you'll have to do it all. You'll have to drag them along.

Be more specific about how you challenged people with goals.

Henderson: Well, we set the goals here at the national level, and then we have a national executive conference each year where we outline the goals and celebrate success stories. We spend a lot of time on recognition, so people get pumped up. It's the equivalent, in my mind, of screaming in a locker room before the start of a football game.

At that meeting, we talk about the challenges of the future, and, by the end of the meeting, people are ready to accept the vision for the coming year—not the numbers, maybe—but certainly the vision. Then we go through a process of playing 'catch,' which is really a negotiations process to arrive at agreement about the numbers that we expect people to make. To sell people on the numbers, we build incentive and bonus plans into the negotiations process. We also outline the factors in the external operating environment that are driving the numbers that we set for performance.

How do the unions feel about what you're doing? Are they behind efforts to become more competitive with the private sector?

Henderson: Well, there's naturally some suspicion at times because management is placing expectations on the union. But we use the same techniques with the unions that we do with management. Essentially, we make a business case for why we need to be competitive. Like the managers, the unions want the Postal Service to succeed, and sometimes we just have to work things through with them until they recognize what we're up against in the marketplace.

I'll give you an example. We outsourced Priority Mail processing centers, as you know. The unions adamantly opposed that. They thought we were selling off work. But we showed them the differential in quality between what these Priority Mail processing centers were able to do and what the Postal Service was doing internally. And they acknowledged that there was a wide gap.

So did the conversation end there?

Henderson: No, they asked us if they could go into that external plant to find out how it was operating, so that they could then bring those approaches back inside. I told them that, if they could figure how to do it as well internally, with the same level of quality and cost per unit, we'd bring it inside again.

So you left the door open?

Henderson: Yes, we agreed to create an internal plant within the Postal Service in which they are now experimenting with new work approaches. As part of this, the unions essentially suspended union rules and operating procedures and are working with us to see if we can replicate that same quality in-house.

This then, is an example of how you're partnering with constituencies inside the Postal Service to drive change and quality improvement.

Henderson: Absolutely. But the key for us was to benchmark. By going outside to a private sector company, we created a new benchmark for the Postal Service. Doing that helped bolster the business case for why it was important that we operate more effectively and at lower cost. The unions bought off on the logic of that.

We've been talking about jobs and how people can work more effi-ciently. About 80 percent of the Postal Service's costs are labor costs. Do you have a sense of how much of your costs should be labor costs versus technology costs? Are future layoffs inevitable as technology becomes even more a part of postal service operations?

Henderson: Well, we're spending about $4 billion a year right now on technology and automation. Roughly half that is for infrastructure re-pair and replacement. We'd like to spend more, but that just isn't fea-sible given the scope and scale of our operations. We need to spend more to bring about the truly widespread changes in our operations that are called for. If you take the printing industry as a surrogate, that industry literally reengineered itself by spending about 20 per-cent of its revenues on reinvestment in technology infrastructure.

Still, the changes we're making, albeit more slowly than we'd like, are making a huge difference, both in how we get things done and the time it takes us to do them. For example, today we can simply download a software change to enhance the recognition ability of cameras in postal facilities. We no longer have to go out and buy new equipment all the time like we did years ago. Things like that are increasing our productivity and cutting costs signifi-cantly. It's also driving the redesign of peoples' jobs.

Let's talk about that. How will advancing technology in postal service operations ultimately impact peoples' jobs?

Henderson: Down the line, it'll ultimately mean most of our plants will be what we call 'lights out' operations. They'll be manned by maintenance people, keeping robots and other pieces of mecha-nization working. That's the direction we're moving in. Our 'test tube' experiment for this kind of operation is in Fort Myers, Florida, where we have a 'lights out' plant. Mail comes in the door by con-veyor and is never touched by people again. It goes through a sorter and is dispatched by robots. Now you have a lot of people there— not the number we have in plants today—but people are there. They're all highly trained electronic technicians. Somebody has got to be on hand to fix this stuff, so it's not a peopleless place. It's just that the people there have different skill sets from what you find in most postal facilities today.

Is this the mail processing plant of the future?

Henderson: Oh, yes. That's why I'm encouraging people nowadays to get into the maintenance area and other technical fields. That's where future postal jobs will be. We have a huge training center in Norman, Oklahoma, probably the largest technical training facility in the world, outside of the military. That facility is preparing people for more and more technical jobs. Instead of unloading trucks, we will need people to adjust optical character readers. People will still be dealing with customers, of course. Robots won't be doing that.

What concerns do postal employees express to you when you go traveling out into the field?

Henderson: Their biggest concerns have to do with how technology will impact them and their jobs. They wonder sometimes if they are dinosaurs. So I talk to them about how technology actually represents a net gain for the Postal Service. I tell them that, if they prepare for the jobs that technology creates, they will have interesting and challenging jobs to do. And we offer lots of good training to help prepare people for the new postal jobs of the future. We have very aggressive general manager training, for example. We collaborate with many top universities to provide people with the latest management techniques. We have satellite training and other things.

So postal employees don't have to worry about job security?

Henderson: Not like people in other industries. I mean, I don't foresee in my lifetime a nation that doesn't require a ubiquitous mail delivery system. I will be long gone from this earth and probably my kids, too, before there's any real substitute in place for actual physical delivery of mail. Nowadays, after all, we use hovercraft to deliver mail in Alaska and mules in the Grand Canyon. Those delivery channels aren't going away anytime soon.

Is it still the goal of the Postal Service to keep all employees for the duration of their careers? Is that still something that the Postal Service worker today should expect?

Henderson: Yes. That's an important cornerstone of our culture. Despite all the transformation taking place in the Postal Service today in terms of its functions, its customer focus, its marketing, and its management, the fact is we want to keep people for the long haul. That means you have to act each and every day to keep the organization healthy and competitive so that jobs can be preserved.

Why keep people for the long term?

Henderson: It fits with our organizational mission. Our mission is to provide high-quality mail delivery, and you need people to do that. Loyal people. Developing a culture of pride and loyalty is critical to us fulfilling our marketing mission, providing consistency of service and ubiquity of service.

That's interesting. The notion of life-long (or even long-term) employment has gone by the wayside in so many industries.

Henderson: That's true. The private sector often uses the metaphor of the 'burning platform' to underscore the need for radical, transformational change in companies. But in my case, I can't stand up in front of people and tell them that mail service is going away. It's not, and I'd look pretty foolish if I took that approach. I have to deal with the hand I've been dealt. In my case, I have to leverage people's pride in and loyalty to this organization as the way to drive changes in how we operate.

Switching gears for a moment, what about the Internet. Threat or opportunity?

Henderson: Huge opportunity. It gives us another channel through which to communicate with customers. Frankly, it gives them an easy way to buy hard goods, which, of course, we'll deliver. Just look at what's already happened with Christmas retail sales. In 1997, Americans did $2.6 billion in Christmas shopping on the Internet. In 1998, they spent $8.6 billion, and the U.S. Postal Service delivered a lot of those goods.

What you're saying, then, is that the emergence of the Internet as a sales channel is going to have a 'multiplier effect' for the Postal Service? It will generate large amounts of collateral revenues as the result of what people order online?

Henderson: Correct. The purchases you make by electronic means still have some sort of hard copy associated with them. Even if you purchase and download new software onto a home computer, there's often still hard copy documentation that gets sent to you.

Bill, as you continue to transform the culture here and build support for your efforts, what do you see as the key challenges for the Postal Service in the short and long term?

Henderson: The biggest challenge we face is with employees. They're the key to our success, but it's very hard to get a new vision into the heads of nearly a million people. We're only as good as the quality of our infrastructure, and our people infrastructure is the main support strut there. So we have to be focused, we need to understand the nature of our future, and we need to drive ourselves to get there.

As we conclude, talk about your personal role as a leader managing change. What makes you effective? What have you most enjoyed about being a change agent?

Henderson: I think one thing that makes me an effective leader is that I know our employees. I like to say that, wherever I go in the U.S., I can walk into a post office and find friends there. So I know our people; I know what makes them tick. I know what their concerns and fears are, but I also know what they're capable of. It's my role to help build people's confidence in being able to perform at high levels. Today we're doing that more effectively than ever, I believe.

In terms of what I enjoy about my job, I'd say simply that it's intellectually challenging. Moreover, the war is never won. Every time you cross the finish line, the gun goes off signaling the start of another race. So the pace of things here is challenging, stimulating, and fun.

Are the challenges you face here at the Postal Service unique to this organization, or are they similar to what any large organization deals with as it goes through transformation?

Henderson: I think we're like most any other large organization. Like other large organizations—General Motors, Ford, and IBM—we've had a tendency to be inward-looking, to live in a cocoon. In today's business environment, though, no organization can afford to operate that way. Nor can we assume we're bulletproof. We're not, just as IBM learned in the 1980s that it was not. We've got to keep alert to what's happening in the external business environment. We've got to focus on our customers and on ourselves to succeed and thrive in the twenty-first century global marketplace for mail services.

Chapter Conclusions

As this chapter reveals, managing change in the Postal Service requires a slightly different leadership model than we've seen in other chapters. For one thing, Bill Henderson has indicated that it is both unrealistic and inappropriate to base the need for change in his organization on the metaphor of the "burning platform." He clearly notes that the Postal Service is not in imminent danger of being overtaken by competitors or eliminated from the marketplace. Thus to transform how the organization operates, he must appeal to postal workers' sense of pride and loyalty as the basis on which their motivation to work differently will rest.

He Gives Employees Confidence

As this interview clearly shows, that strategy has worked. Henderson has emboldened managers with an enhanced sense of self-confidence and the knowledge that they hold it within their zone of control to improve organizational performance. But it hasn't been through personal exhortation alone. Henderson has made strong use of incentives and performance evaluation procedures to drive new ways of working. Equally important, he has gone out of his way to make sure the Postal Service celebrates "small victories" on the way to enhancing its overall performance. As any effective change leader knows, recognition is an extremely important way to build momentum (and employee commitment) for organizational change.

Henderson is clearly a leader who springs from the very ranks of those he now oversees. His ability to lead relies on a combination of experimentation, exhortation, communication, and a common touch—all of which combine to create a highly effective leadership style with a group of individuals long accustomed to organizational stability.

So what are the lessons that emerge from this chapter that could potentially be leveraged elsewhere?

- **Keep communicating.** Clearly, Henderson puts a premium on the importance of communications as the basis of his own leadership effectiveness. In this regard, he is much like Lee Griffin, CEO of Bank One of Louisiana, who recognizes that spending time among the troops is often the most effective way to leverage change.

- **Identify with the rank-and-file.** Like Griffin, Henderson also eschews the leadership pedestal, preferring to see himself as one of his organization's rank and file. During our interview, for example, Henderson took obvious pride in speaking about the loyalty of today's Postal Service employees. It's a feeling one would not see displayed in every corporate leader today or even in most of those profiled in this book.

- **See change as a continuous journey.** Another lesson that one can draw from this chapter is that change is a continuous journey, and it makes tremendous personal, intellectual, and leadership demands of leaders. Toward the end of our interview, Henderson remarked about how the change "battle" is never won. There is always a *next* battle to be waged, new hurdles to overcome on the way to achieving and completing organizational transformation.

- **Be pragmatic yet visionary.** Perhaps the most salient thing to emerge from our interview with Bill Henderson has to do with his pragmatism. Although his own personal and family roots are deeply ensconced in postal service tradition, he clearly understands that the business environment in which the Postal Service operates today is a far cry from what his own father knew not that many years ago.

Far from being a romantic, Henderson is the ultimate pragmatist, able to energize employees even as he presents them with new performance expectations. In many ways a charismatic leader, Henderson is also a clear-headed one. He knows that if postal service traditions are to continue to be established, the very nature of how the Postal Service functions must change in response to the increasingly competitive business environment in which it operates.

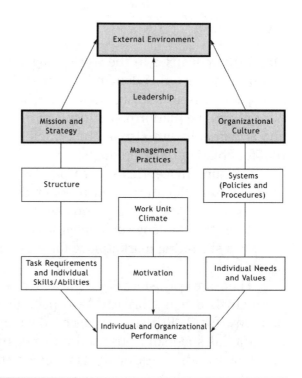

9 Managing Growth in a Shrinking Marketplace: How British Aerospace is Reinventing Itself for the Next Century

"The race for technological improvement drives on two levels at once: improving the product itself and improving the processes by which it is made. On one level, engineers add refinements and complexity to their product while, on the other level, they try to extract time and cost from the design and manufacturing processes. The new industrial leaders are those brilliantly managed firms that do both simultaneously . . ."

—William Greider, *One World, Ready or Not*

Of all the industries in the world today, few can rival the product complexity, customer demands, or marketplace competitiveness of aerospace. It is an industry that relies heavily on high technology, not only as the platform and inspiration for new weapons systems and armaments, but also as the principal design and development tool for creating those products.

Like pharmaceuticals, aerospace is an industry that requires huge capital allocations and product development cycles of ten years or more. And it is an industry that, in the wake of the Cold War, faces the challenge of managing continued business growth in what is a shrinking marketplace for weapons of war and defensive capability.

There are only a few major players in aerospace, one of the most distinguished being British Aerospace (BAe). BAe is a company of many firsts. British Aerospace developed the first and only operational supersonic transport plane, the Concorde. BAe also developed the revolutionary Harrier jet, the first vertical/short-takeoff-and-landing fighter that has seen service in a variety of operating theaters, including the Gulf War.

A Company with a Distinguished Pedigree

The antecedents of present-day BAe have equally distinguished pedigrees. It was The Supermarine Works, part of present-day BAe, that developed the legendary Spitfire, which saw long and highly successful use in World War II. And it was de Havilland Aviation, another antecedent company, that produced the famous de Havilland Mosquito. Known as the "Wooden Wonder" because of its all-wood construction, the Mosquito saw legendary service as a light bomber in the European Air War between 1939 and 1945.

Today, British Aerospace is a major aerospace and engineering firm employing 43,000 people and with annual sales of more than $14 billion, 89 percent of which is overseas. A pioneer and leader of major international collaborative projects involving 29 nations, it is Europe's major proven systems integrator. It produces and markets a full array of armaments and weapons systems, from military air-craft, naval combat systems, and sonar to the most advanced guided weapons and small arms. BAe also advises nations on force structure and how to plan for military conflicts in various geopolitical settings, blending the use of air, sea, and land weapons capabilities. BAe is also a major shareholder in Airbus Industrie.

A New Need to Compete on a Global Stage

But providing such highly complex services to clients is a demanding task requiring highly refined production processes, effective internal organizational coordination, and strong collaborative work approaches. It's made doubly difficult in a shrinking defense industry marketplace where BAe must compete increasingly with companies like Boeing and Lockheed Martin, both of whom bring huge scale and technical capabilities to the competitive table.

Hence, British Aerospace, along with three other principal aerospace companies—France's Aerospatiale; Spain's Casa; and Germany's Daimler-Benz Aerospace—agreed in principle in 1998 to attempt the process of forming a unified aviation and defense company. If the endeavor succeeds, it will create a European megacompany with the economic muscle and organizational scale to compete with Boeing and Lockheed on a global basis.

Against this backdrop, Sir Richard Evans, Chairman of British Aerospace, has been working hard since his ascendancy to the helm of BAe in 1990 to create a more responsive, more unified, and more customer-focused company. But it hasn't been easy.

Formerly a Collection of "Independent Fiefdoms"

Part of the reason stems from BAe's distinguished history. Until Evans came on the scene in the 1990s, BAe operated as a federation of "fiercely independent fiefdoms," the 1977 merger of various British aircraft companies to form a nationalized BAe, never having resulted in a strong unified corporate entity.

We caught up with Evans in his office to talk with him about the challenges he has faced as Chairman of British Aerospace. We spoke about the need he faced, in 1992, to oversee the largest corporate write-off in U.K. industrial history—£1 billion—in order to position the company to be competitive on a going-forward basis. We then talked about how he began the process, now five years in the making, of bringing about a large-gauge culture change at BAe by introducing something called the "BAe Benchmark Program." Conceived at the very top of the organization, this program has involved an arduous process of redrafting the company's mission statement and forging five critical business values to guide the company into the twenty-first century:

1.   PEOPLE are our greatest strength.

2.   CUSTOMERS are our highest priority.

3.   PARTNERSHIPS are our future.

4.   INNOVATION and TECHNOLOGY are our competitive edge.

5.   PERFORMANCE is the key to winning.

To win support for these values, Evans had to secure management buy-in at multiple levels in the organization. Today, the company's new mission statement and new business values form the basis for an increasingly collaborative and team-oriented corporate culture that is taking root at BAe, and which Evans sees as essential as BAe speeds toward economic integration with other European defense industry players.

We pick up our conversation with Evans talking about the challenges he has faced in bringing about broad-based culture change within BAe.

Back in 1992, Dick, you faced major challenges in positioning BAe to be globally competitive. The company had acquired a lot of liabilities over the years, which you got rid of through the largest corporate write-off in U.K. industrial history. You then began the process of looking around for models of other companies that had transitioned from being public sector entities to private sector firms. Talk about that experience and what came from it.

Evans: After taking the write-off and making other changes, including selling off the Rover motorcar company (The Rover Group) in 1994, I wanted to find examples of companies that had been through the kinds of challenges we'd been through, and that led me to British Airways, among others. BA, of course, had been privatized and had its own change challenges to deal with (see Chapter 6). I spoke with John King (the Chairman at the time) and Colin Marshall, and it was through talking with them that I recognized we needed to undertake a large-scale change program if we were to move the company into the future and change the way we interrelated with one another within the company.

Why was a large-scale change program in order for BAe?

Evans: From the late 1970s, when it was formed, through the early 1990s, BAe remained a collection of different companies that, prior to the formation of the business, had been fierce competitors with one another. This was getting in our way of being a single unified company.

For example, employees didn't talk about British Aerospace. Instead, they talked about de Havilland, or, if you went up to Manchester, they talked about A.V. Rowe. If you went someplace else, they talked about the Bristol Aeroplane Company or Vickers. It was almost as if British Aerospace, as an entity, was a kind of distant cousin whom you encountered every so often in your travels, but there was no allegiance to the entity called British Aerospace.

So you determined that you had to find ways to bring everyone inside the company together around a common set of values and goals, correct? How did you do that?

Evans: Well, it involved several steps. I recognized that, if we were to be successful in the future, we had to get buy-in from all our people for a new way of working and a new way of thinking. This would be essential for success. We had to come together as a single company. We couldn't afford to be a collection of independent entities anymore all competing with one another.

So over a number of months, I held discussions with members of the BAe board of management (the top internal executive team reporting directly to Evans). We came up with a vision for the business, which became the basis for establishing a set of values as well as a new mission statement.

These discussions took about six months to get to a point we all felt comfortable with. It then became apparent that we needed to expand these discussions to include a larger group of people in the organization, and this is what we did. We brought the next group of managers in the organization—a group of 30—into our discussions. And, in essence, we began the discussion process about our vision and values all over again. The new group interrogated us, often in a hostile way, about why we'd come up with the values we'd identified. They questioned the order, sequence, and priority we'd given to them. It took us another three months to get through this larger group of executives before we felt sufficiently comfortable to expand the group again.

We then extended the group of 30 to include all the key executives. This became known as the 'Group of 130.' This group became the 'engine room' to first discuss and challenge our work and, ultimately, to support and drive rollout of our change efforts.

Was there resistance every time you expanded the number of people taking part in this dialogue about values?

Evans: Absolutely! Each time I expanded the discussion group, there were those in the existing group who didn't want to do it. And when we did include new people, they always grilled us about the values we'd come up with and would want to go back to the very beginning and start afresh to discuss still other potential values and business goals before we got to any form of consensus or buy-in. All this took a great deal of time. We began the process in 1994, and it wasn't until the beginning of 1999 that we got to the point where some 170 of us felt confident about taking it forward. You can see, therefore, that it took us a long time to achieve the buy-in, but we believed it was essential to have.

Why do you think it was such an arduous process?

Evans: Well, we started off with five people who were a natural work team—the board of management. These were guys who worked together in their normal day jobs. And to some extent, that natural work team applied to the first group of 15 that we initially added to the group.

When we went beyond that group of 20, however, we started incorporating into our conversations people who didn't work together every day and who weren't necessarily a natural work team. A lot of these guys, despite the fact that they'd worked for their respective part of the company for 20 or 25 years, had never met one another before. People were suspicious. There was a constant process of building trust before we could move forward.

Really?

Evans: Yes. And as we brought larger and larger groups of people together for these discussions, people reacted in different ways. Some people reacted very positively. For example, a lot of people were pleased to find others in the organization that thought just as they did about things, who wanted to see change take place and who wanted to be part of that change. But at the other end of the spectrum, there were people who were very uncomfortable about sharing information or knowledge inside the organization. Knowledge was power, and we were taking this from them and breaking down the walls that separated the different parts of the organization. And we were. That was our intent!

So some people felt very threatened by the discussion process?
Evans: Of course! Because we *were* breaking down the walls, sharing knowledge among large groups of people who, in many cases, didn't know each other and hadn't worked together before. We had some very difficult and very acrimonious discussions as we met as a larger and larger group to talk about business values and the need to drive the Benchmark Program forward.

As these meetings progressed, you used a professional facilitator to guide the discussions and to keep people on task. What role did you personally play as these group meetings took place?
Evans: I presented myself as the owner of this program. So I attended each and every program session we held, and I devoted a large amount of my time to it. I also did it in a very visible way. People had to see and believe that I was personally committed.

What did you do in these sessions?
Evans: We organized and ran a series of highly structured workshops. There was an enormous amount of preparation required. Each workshop had a clear agenda and a specific set of objectives. Generally, they were run over two days, which included either one or two evenings.

Intially, there was a general belief that the program would not last, that I'd tire of it and life would then return to 'normal.' The more they saw me putting a large amount of my own time into the workshops, however, the more everyone began to believe it was something that was for real. I kept telling them, 'I know you guys think I'm going to get off this, but I'm not; it's too important. This is going to go on for years and years, and I'm not going to stop talking about it.' For the first two or three years, I played a very active role in every single workshop and in the preparation and planning of them.

What happened in these workshops? Did people engage around the idea of forging a new set of values for the organization?

Evans: Eventually they did, but I got a lot of pushback from people. People asked, 'Why do we need to do this? We're operating perfectly well. We all have big change programs to deal with in our own businesses. Why the hell do we need to do all this other stuff?' Many seriously thought and believed that I had some sort of hidden agenda and simply wanted to be told what to do so they could go away and do it.

What finally made people realize you were serious about bringing about change in the organization and using these discussion groups and workshop sessions to do it?

Evans: After one particularly difficult workshop, I seriously thought we were in danger of losing the whole Benchmark Program. I knew that we were at a make-or-break point. A radical move was required to reenergize the program, and it had to get everyone's attention so that there could be no doubting my own commitment to delivering the Benchmark Program. I decided to immediately move one of our key executives, Kevin Smith, who was, at the time, running the biggest of our businesses, the military aircraft company. I told him, 'Kevin, come Monday morning, I'm taking you out of your job. You're no longer going to be the Managing Director of the military aircraft company. I'm making you the Manager of the BAe Benchmark Program on a full-time basis.' To my relief, he agreed to do it.

That had an electrifying effect on people. People suddenly realized, 'Gosh, if this guy is going to take the guy who's head of the biggest business unit and move him into the Benchmark Program job, then he's really serious about using this process to bring about change.'

It sent a very strong signal to people that you were serious about driving change in the organization. It wasn't just lip service or hot air.

Evans: Absolutely! I also went to every one of our businesses and got the resumes of the 20 or so brightest young managers between the ages of 26 and 36. I took this whole group of people out of their businesses and relocated them for a year to group headquarters.

We took these young people and allocated them equally to the five values. We then created value teams under the leadership of the executive directors and allocated each of these young people as facilitators for these teams. They worked with the value leaders in creating tools and techniques to support use of the values in workshops. They also became staffers who did all the hands-on facilitation work associated with our in-house discussion of the business values. I knew that, as they moved on in their careers, these people would be stalwart supporters of the Benchmark Program on a going-forward basis.

Now just as Kevin Smith's appointment to head up the program had sent a strong message to employees, the redeployment of many of the company's best and brightest young graduates for an entire year to work on the program sent a big message out to the organization, as well. These people were hugely enthusiastic, so they brought an enormous amount of energy and momentum to the discussion process, especially as we opened it up to more and more people.

By this time, too, we were beginning to develop projects as an output of each of the value workshops we were running. These had to be managed, just like any significant business project within the company would be managed. So these people were intimately involved with that task. They had a huge effect on driving the program forward. They made me realize that the further down in the organization you go to find allies for change, the more enthusiastic the people are. Conversely, obstruction to change is always at the top of the organization, where people feel they have the most to give up.

Let's talk about some of the projects and programs that began to emerge from the workshop and discussion process. What kinds of things were outputs of these sessions? In what ways did they reflect the new corporate values you were espousing?

Evans: There are some clear examples. For instance, we implemented 360-degree reporting throughout all management levels of the company, which then led us to the most difficult thing we've done so far, which is peer-group assessments. We also spent a good deal of time developing metrics by which to measure our success in completing projects and tasks associated with each of the values.

To come up with appropriate measures, we took teams of people outside the company to look at other organizations that were doing things similar to us. We identified companies like Hewlett-Packard and Coca-Cola that we wanted to study in terms of their best practices. We started taking groups of managers and executives out to these companies. We discovered that many of the problems we were having with operationalizing the introduction of our values were similar to those that these other companies had struggled with.

So this was a kind of benchmarking and reality-test exercise that you undertook?

Evans: Yes. What we were doing through this action was creating the measurements we needed to put in place as we began the process of really changing how we worked. We needed to identify benchmark practices with respect to each of the values and then create a set of measurements by which we could identify and constantly measure ourselves to see whether we were making progress.

As a result of this field work, we introduced two key techniques into our management practices: First, we introduced the measurement standards of the European Foundation of Quality Management (EFQM) into our business processes. Then we created a major training program to train facilitators in all our businesses so that we could implement EFQM standards throughout the company. Second, we instituted a peer-group assessment process, which I mentioned earlier. Everyone in the group of 170 was assessed by a minimum of 25 and a maximum of 30 of his peers from the group. We began this back at the start of 1998, and it took about three months to complete. This assessment program was highly detailed. We had question sets that dealt with each of the five values. And each piece of the assessment evaluated individuals on their performance relative to each of the values. Each of us took the assessment, using an intranet-based tool that had grown out of the work done by one of our values teams.

Why did you do this assessment?

Evans: Because we wanted to have a measure that would help us identify how effectively we were seen by our peers to have adopted the values to which we had agreed. Ratings ran from 'A' at the top to 'E' at the bottom for each value, from which a league table was effectively created. This was a very difficult period for all involved. Some individuals simply could not come to terms with the results. Others asked for and received help to overcome their own deficiencies as seen by their peer group.

It sounds like the assessment has proven a powerful tool in helping identify which of peoples' behaviors were in sync with the new values and which were not.

Evans: Yes. We've also been working with a team of industrial psychologists who were initially working with the entire group of 170 and, subsequently, others as well. Starting with the board of management, we have each taken complete psychological assessments so that we all understand our own work behaviors better. At first, there was an awful lot of fear associated with this, until we began to realize how valuable a tool it was for understanding human motivations and actions in the organization. Now these activities are accepted as normal process.

Fascinating. How did you overcome people's quite understandable fears about taking this kind of psychological profile exam?

Evans: Well, the executive directors and I were the first to take it. This gets to a principle of mine that I think is key if you're going to lead an organization: never ask anybody to do anything that you aren't prepared to do yourself. So along with the other four executives on the board, I went off for three days to commence this activity. In three days, I learned more about myself and about the guys I worked with than I'd learned in the whole time I'd been working with them up to then, and I think this applied to all of us.

What kinds of things did you learn about yourself?

Evans: Well, I learned a lot about my own psychological makeup and why I act and react in the ways I do. A lot goes back to patterns formed in one's adolescent years. So if you can understand those patterns in an explicit and mature way, it's helpful as you interact with others in the workplace.

So becoming aware of your own behaviors and style of interacting with others proved very valuable as you and the board have driven change at BAe?

Evans: Definitely.

Now you're extending this peer-group assessment process else-where in the organization, correct? Others are now getting the chance to do the kind of in-depth psychological assessment that you and members of the board had, right?

Evans: Correct.

You obviously think it's important that people understand their own behaviors better if they're to change how they work with others in the company. Have people objected to doing this assessment work? Have they complained that it is too 'touchy-feely?'

Evans: Of course. Initially, it's extremely difficult. People are afraid of it. This is why bringing about change—any kind of change—in an organization takes so long. You can't make any moves until you make people comfortable with what you want to do. That isn't to say everybody will be with you. In any large group, you're always going to have a small number who can't face up to change. They may pay lip service to the importance of what you're doing but not believe any of it. These people are identified by their own peer group and by the body language they display when they walk out the door and go back to their workplace. In the end, however, they become an irrelevant minority. Most depart because of it.

We've been talking a lot about the internal activities you undertook to drive change here at BAe. How are the changes that you're making internally affecting how you deal with customers? Moreover, what has been the benefit to the bottom-line?

Evans: Well, we were about three years into our Benchmark Program when Kevin Smith, who I mentioned earlier, came up to me at the end of one of the workshops and said that he and the 170 group had identified some serious deliverables. The group committed themselves to delivering a billion pounds of cash improvement to the business plan, and they did it.

How did the workshops and change activities that you'd been conducting help drive the achievement of those business results?

Evans: Out of the workshops came the belief that, by delivering on the values, we'd contribute tremendously to the financial health of the business. For example, consider all the conversations we had around the value of *innovation* and *technology*. One thing the workshops did was make us realize that, when it came to best practices, we already had a wealth of best practices within the company. They were scattered all over the company but were not being shared. So we made it a priority to start sharing best practices more effectively inside the company.

Consider all the conversations we had around the value of *customers.* All those discussions helped people to understand that the largest number of customers we had weren't outside the company but actually *inside* it! We have annual revenues of some eight or nine billion pounds a year, but the number of external customers we have is tiny. It's probably about 200. Inside the company, however, we probably have 30,000 customers, people who rely on others inside the company for delivery.

Is it fair to say that the relationships you have with these internal customers are what determine the quality of the relationships you have with external customers?

Evans: Absolutely. At the end of the day, the value the external customer gets from British Aerospace is entirely dependent on the sum and the parts that we create *inside* the business. Here's an example: Picture a billet of material—aluminum—coming into our goods receiving department. That billet of material goes into a machine shop, where someone, an individual, starts machining parts out of metal planks. He has to create a given number of parts that then go into a kit of parts. And when that kit of parts gets sent up the line to someone else, who starts the assembly process, there might be a hundred pieces in it. But if even one part is missing, the kit is useless. It can't be assembled. Since that's the case, the person who cuts the metal to make the parts has a customer who is the person who has to assemble them.

Before we had these values, our people never thought of themselves as each others' customers. Indeed, there was no such thing as an internal customer. But through the values, we began to realize that our business success with external customers relied on us seeing one another as customers at various points in our research, development, manufacturing, and assembly processes.

So the workshops stimulated breakthrough thinking around new ways to work, and now that message has gotten down to the plant and manufacturing floor?

Evans: Well, we're getting there. As of September 1998, we'd gotten the discussions about values down to all 1,500 executives within British Aerospace. That's the whole of our management chain. And from there, the real rollout of the program has had to start with the 45,000 employees of the company. All 1,500 executives have had to go through special training to deliver the values down into the masses of people working in the organization. We've been working at this for five years, and, in effect, we have only just begun to start the complete rollout process! We are now at the most critical part of the program, and we have been for the last six months, as we move to introduce our values-based work approaches into the big battalions of the company.

Why is now an especially critical time for change efforts here?

Evans: Because when you're dealing with a team of 170 guys, you can manage the process. Not easily, but you can do it. And you have a very close relationship with them. The further down the management chain you go, however, the more distant the chain becomes, and the more dependent you are on the middle and junior managers of the organization.

So maintaining momentum is the most important thing at this point?

Evans: Certainly. The way we'll know if we're being successful is to measure the performance of our managers by doing future attitude surveys with employees. We do a people survey every two years, but in the intervening years, we do very detailed sampling survey work on specific issues.

In the past, employees have rated BAe managers badly. They've said things like, 'Managers don't understand the problems we have and don't communicate with us well.' So, now, as part of our change program, some of a manager's bonus is linked to the improved ratings they get from employees in our surveys.

We've identified a number of issues critical to how managers act toward employees generally. Managers, for example, have to really focus on helping people work together to solve business problems. I've made it clear to managers and executives that we must see improvements—specific improvements in how managers are judged. 'If you get the ratings,' I've told people, 'this is what you'll get. If you don't make the grade, we've got a problem.'

It's a powerful way to motivate managers to work differently. But it also sends a message to rank-and-file employees, doesn't it?

Evans: Yes. It's just one of the tools we're using to focus people's minds. This isn't lip service. Managers really have to go out and deliver on the values and behave in accordance with them. What's more, they have to be seen and judged by the people who are working for them to be doing so.

What are the other ways you're driving alignment with change efforts at this time?

Evans: Well, we're extending 360-degree reporting elsewhere in the organization. We're also putting a lot of investment into education and training. As part of the BAe Benchmark Program, we've established a virtual university, and we're putting a lot more emphasis on continuous learning. I sometimes tell employees, 'Look, you don't just come into the company, get a job, and then stop learning. This is a constant process.'

If we want that to happen, though, we have to provide people with the tools to enable them to actually think and behave more intelligently. We don't want people working a lot harder, but we do want them working more intelligently.

Dick, you're now five years into the transformation process. What are the challenges or bumps in the road that you think could still lie ahead?

Evans: Number one is complacency. As we begin to produce good results, it's easy for people to sit back and think, 'Well, we've done it.' That's not true.

What happens is that, as we make progress in certain areas, our competition in the marketplace is simply mobilized into action, working harder than ever to try and overtake us. So complacency is an enemy we have to be very watchful for.

Second, the test now is to get all 45,000 British Aerospace employees to sign up to our new values—people, customers, partnerships, innovation and technology, and performance—and behave in accordance with these values and with the 1,500 executives who we have already locked into the program. If this doesn't work all through the organization, then we've lost.

Talk more about the specific (and concrete) results you've already achieved through your culture change efforts.

Evans: One big change we've seen is that people are now talking with one another across all parts of the organization. I'll give you an example. Recently, we decided to exit from the turboprop market. For this part of our business, this created a big problem in terms of downsizing and shedding labor. Hitherto, the Managing Director of that particular business would have dealt with the problem with little help from the rest of the organization.

I was speaking to the guy a couple of days after the announcement to see how he was coping, and he told me he was doing fine. It turns out that virtually every other Managing Director in the company had already rung him to say, 'Let us know what skills the displaced workers have, and we'll see if we can match some of those to the jobs we have. We'll try to solve part of the problem for you, rather than you having to shed them onto the redundancy heap and put them out of the company.'

Well, before we started the Benchmark BAe Program, I don't believe that guy would have had a single call from anybody in any other business in the company. We were so siloed in how we operated, and the walls between the individual business were so high.

So BAe is really moving toward being a more fluid and 'boundaryless' organization, just as you've pushed for?
Evans: Yes.

Do you see this move toward being a more boundaryless organization as a way to more effectively leverage intellectual capital inside the company?
Evans: Absolutely. I see it as giving us a lot more flexibility in sharing knowledge. It also gives our people a real sense of identity—and gives British Aerospace a sense of identity, as well. That's important. I want people to be identified by their behaviors. I want customers outside this company to say, 'That is British Aerospace behavior.' That is what I expect people here to strive for.

How will the new behaviors that British Aerospace employees are beginning to exhibit be useful as the company positions itself for success in the global defense industry marketplace in the future?
Evans: Well, for one thing, we're beginning to get good at cross-functional work and cooperation. We're not yet where a company like GE is, but we're developing what I believe will be a very

powerful competitive tool that we'll be able to use to meet our customers' needs. We now have processes in place whose effectiveness and efficiency we can measure, so we'll be able to tell if we're getting better, standing still, or getting worse. And this new set of skills represents real value for us. When we go into partnership with other companies or pursue merger activities, these skills will be highly transferable. In fact, we're already getting accolades from companies about the new ways in which we're working both internally and with customers and suppliers.

It sounds as if developing these competencies will also be of value to BAe as it looks toward greater integration of the European defense industry. Is that true?

Evans: There's no doubt of that. I believe there's going to be a lot more integration of the industry across Europe. That's something we must continue to work toward. Here in Europe, there's simply too much capacity. On a going-forward basis, the industry is not sufficiently profitable to generate the investment that is required to maintain and grow the technology base. So we simply must become more integrated as an industry to support technological development, which can only come from increased profitability.

Further, when you look at the distribution of our markets between Europe and North America, it's very important that North American companies be challenged in order to keep their own competitive edge. This is what drives any business forward, and I think we are very much positioning ourselves to do that.

There's still another reason we have to be able to work in a fluid sort of way as a company today. We have a lot of relationships in America and a lot of partnerships there. We're partners in programs with Lockheed. We're partners in programs with Boeing. And we have partnership agreements with AlliedSignal, Raytheon, and others. Those companies want to be partnered with top-quality companies from the European side. They don't want to be partnered with a second-rate organization any more than we want to be partnered with second-rate organizations in America. And this applies to the rest of the world, as well.

One last question: It seems to us that you're a big believer in the idea of the 'leader as learner.' From the 360-degree assessments you've done, to the workshops BAe has conducted to drive culture change, to the efforts you've made along with members of your senior management team to better understand how individually you all interact with one another, there's a lot of emphasis on learning as critical to the change process. Is that a fair assessment?

Evans: Definitely. When you're leading change efforts, you simply must be open to new learning every step along the way. Moreover, you can't ask anybody to do anything that you yourself aren't willing to do first. If I'm not prepared to do something, then I don't think it's reasonable to expect others to do it. For me, it is part of the buy-in process. If you want people to buy in to what it is you want to do, you've got to first demonstrate that you're willing to put yourself out there as a guinea pig. You've got to be willing to say to people, 'Hey, look. I am prepared to set the example and go out and acquire the tool kit of new skills and behaviors I need to be successful. I expect you to do the same.' That's the way you get broad-based organizational buy-in for a change effort, by setting yourself up as an example and then asking others to follow you. That's what leadership is all about.

Chapter Conclusions

As this chapter reveals, Dick Evans is busily involved in bringing significant culture change to British Aerospace. And while his efforts as CEO clearly have been the chief catalyst of change, this chapter reveals some of the "nuances" that are often integral to the most successful of change efforts: the importance of managing change on multiple fronts inside an organization, making these efforts as contiguous as possible, and establishing a clear *need* for a company to change.

He Built a Circle of Support for Change

As a CEO, Evans didn't operate in isolation. To succeed, he involved successively larger groups of key executives, managers, and process owners in a continually expanding dialogue about the company's values and how those values could best be operationalized at the job, workplace, and process level. It was at times an arduous process, one that required nearly five years of work, but one that Evans views as having been critical "foundation-building" for subsequent change to occur.

Evans also made a compelling case for change very early on in BAe's transformation process, which proved a galvanizing ingredient in propelling change efforts forward. He asked John Weston (then Managing Director of BAe's Military Aircraft unit and now CEO of BAe) to conduct an environmental scan with particular emphasis on examining competitor activities and what was happening in the aviation and aerospace industry worldwide. The picture that emerged from John's report, which was that the existing performance levels of BAe business units were inadequate to deal with emergent competitive threats in the aerospace industry environment, created a sense of urgency within Evans and the management board to bring changes to how BAe operated. From this point onward, change efforts essentially cascaded through the organization, following a deliberate and systematic route to transformation.

To assist Evans in managing BAe's transformation process, Bob Bauman, formerly CEO of SmithKline Beecham (see Chapter 4), was brought in to serve as nonexecutive Chairman of the BAe Board of Directors for about a three-year period. Having considerable experience as a change leader, he coached and advised Evans. And as one sees from this chapter's interview, Evans took on the mantle of change leadership with great skill, verve, and dedication. Working as a team, these two leaders provided powerful direction and force to BAe's change efforts. Team-building for the top management group also played a critical role in strengthening team leadership of the effort.

Starting at the top and gradually involving some 170 top managers in BAe, Evans and Bauman built an ever-widening circle of sponsorship and support for change, involving all members of this group in the crafting of a new mission statement for BAe, which, once in place, provided greater clarity for the company's strategy.

Almost concurrent with the crafting of a new mission statement, top BAe managers determined a working set of five values for the company—all of which became support struts for the creation of a new BAe culture.

Even as top company executives were crafting a new identity for BAe by focusing on such important "identity-building" issues as leadership, mission, strategy, and culture, work was also underway to drive change at the deeper transactional and operational levels within the company.

For example, the multirater evaluation process, which we discussed with Evans at length in the interview, helped to instill at a behavioral level the importance of the new business values. It provided the basis for both assessing the appropriateness of people's behaviors at any given moment in time and for benchmarking the company's progress in changing peoples' behavior *over time*. Evans noted this when he talked about how he and other board members decided to undertake the 360-degree feedback process on a regular basis.

The launching of BAe's quality project (based on EFQM) also helped to ensure that the values relating to customers and innovation and technology became integral to business processes at a research, development, and manufacturing level in the company.

Finally, changes in BAe's performance appraisal and reward system helped to reinforce the business values of people and performance when it came to how people did their everyday work. The stress here, of course, was on measurement and recognition, coupled with significant bonuses for high individual performance.

Evans made a brilliant move in selecting one of his key line executives (Kevin Smith) to "take a staff job" and devote himself full time to change implementation efforts. Adding powerfully to this was the selection of many of the company's "best and brightest" to work with Smith. Both steps telegraphed the critical importance of BAe's change efforts to the rest of the employee population.

Also, by making himself the principal "owner" of the change process (at the very beginning), Evans drove his organization to a new awareness that the overwhelming majority of BAe's customers were internal. As a consequence, silos crumbled, and boundaries became more permeable. This step became, in retrospect, a defining moment in the life of BAe and the management team.

In sum, three lessons emerge from the BAe story:

- **The importance of strong leadership to any change effort**

- **The importance of beginning the change process by focusing first on critical "identity" factors in the life of an organization** (in BAe's case: leadership, mission and strategy, and culture—all transformational factors)

- **Finally, the importance of following a conceptual plan to actually implement change, the most difficult single aspect of any change effort.** The work that BAe did at a "transactional" level to secure, fortify, and operationalize strategic decisions made at higher levels has clearly been important to the company's continuing success in a brutally competitive marketplace.

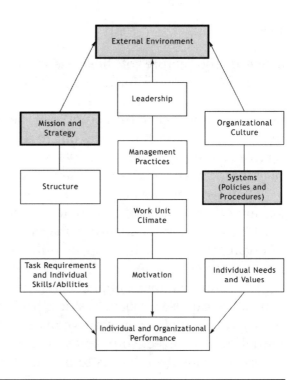

---

10 Let "Service to Customers" Drive Your Company's Structure

"If the 1980s were about quality, and the 1990s were about reengineering, then the 2000s will be about velocity."

—Bill Gates, *Business@ The Speed of Thought*

Ten years ago, who would have imagined that the Internet would emerge as a popular and even preferred conduit through which companies would do business with each other and with retail customers today? Yet judging by the amount of money people spent on the Internet during the 1998 Christmas season ($8.6 billion) as well as by the $300 billion in e-business that companies are expected to be doing over the net by 2002, it's clear that the Internet has already changed the nature of business-to-business and business-to-consumer commerce for all time. Moreover, the roaring performance of Internet stocks on the Nasdaq today suggests abundant business confidence in the potential of the Internet to do even more in the future: to push products out to as-yet-unknown markets, to service customers in bold new ways, to act as a highly responsive sales, marketing, and customer-service channel, and much more.

Yet just how good is *your* company at leveraging the Internet (or any other technology, for that matter) to serve your business needs? The history of change management is littered with stories of organizations that have spent millions on technology only to never see the technology produce the results they expect.

The Internet, for example, represents a powerful new tool that companies can use to boost business performance and differentiate themselves in highly competitive marketplaces. But for its full potential to be realized, companies must make carefully considered decisions about the role it is to play in their business strategy, organizational design, and marketing mix. Moreover, because technology costs are high (and rising every day), it's essential that such decisions be made in the context of a strategic change management framework that links choices about information technologies (IT) to all other operations and components within an organization.

Because use of the Internet and related technologies is evolving so quickly as a component of organizational design today, this chapter provides "mini case-studies" of three companies using technology to support their business strategies. In each case, technology is shaping how the organization operates at a "transactional" level to serve customers, and continuously morphs itself in response to changing customer and marketplace requirements.

Using Technology to Support Business Strategy

In our work with clients, we've found that the companies making best use of the Internet today as a component of their organizational design do so by focusing not on technology per se but on *strategy;* specifically on strategies relating to customer care.[1]

In a recent study, for example, we identified 12 companies that are high performers in the area of customer care and 6 that are clearly customer care "superstars."[2] Each of these companies views customer care as a powerful, competitive differentiator and sees IT as the bridge to getting there. Thus they use "enabling" technologies—computer-telephony integration (CTI), data warehousing, the Internet, and company intranets—not just to sell products and services, but also as a means to build long-term customer relationships, enhance customer loyalty and satisfaction, collect information about competitors, and gather other information that can be used to improve products and business processes on a continuous basis.

Creating Transparency

Each of the customer care "superstars" we identified in this study has used a combination of strategy and technology to structure how it operates. For example, through use of technology, each has effectively integrated scattered and inconsistent customer databases and has transparently tied together geographically and organizationally dispersed customer care operations.

Each has eliminated the problem of incomplete or dated product and service records, which are common in customer service environments. Instead of relying on paper records or isolated computer profiles in customer transactions, each puts such information online and updates it on a continuous, real-time basis. Each makes accountability a major focus of its customer care efforts by putting systems and training in place to support comprehensive account management, upgraded sales, and expeditious resolution of customer complaints. Finally, each has created a "value maximizing network" (of technology, people, and organizational processes) inside its organization that promotes real-time enterprise-wide information sharing (see "Where is Your Company on the Customer Care Continuum?" p. 170).

Customer Service Is a Contact Sport

The customer care "superstars" in our study use every contact with customers as an opportunity to build and enhance customer relationships. How? By systematically capturing information that is used to improve not just customer service but also everything else the company does.

For example, information about manufacturing defects and design problems as well as new product ideas and competitive information is routinely and systematically captured by front-line telephone representatives as they talk to customers. It is then routed on a real-time basis, not just to everybody else who interacts with customers (for example, people in sales or service) but also to others in the organization with a need to know—people in marketing, manufacturing, engineering, and new-product development who are in a position to resolve design problems, create new products and services, or develop new marketing approaches.

USAA: Echoing Customer Calls

To enhance its customer care operations, USAA, an insurance and financial services company with $55 billion in owned and managed assets, built a sophisticated computer system that serves as a high-tech "backbone," linking seven regional call centers and ensuring that customers receive seamless service. At USAA, customer-service reps are specialized by line of business. To support the company's market research and customer care objectives, the company's computer system provides phone reps with parallel access to product and customer databases on local area networks within the company, wide area networks, and on legacy computer systems.

While USAA reps can access customer and product databases from anywhere within the company, the company's regional offices help to foster the perception of a "local presence" in the minds of people who call in. Customer "identifiers" further personalize the calling experience for customers, while related customers are cross-referenced, enabling sales reps to pursue the full range of member needs.

USAA's ECHO ("Every Contact Has Opportunity") approach to dealing with customers uses every contact as a "listening post" with which USAA telephone representatives probe and delve into what is on customers' minds. Through such contacts, USAA's 6,000 sales/service reps can discern emerging market trends, gather competitive information, generate new product ideas, and deal with customers' complaints, notes Julio Alfaro, USAA's department head for member relations and feedback.

When the company gets a customer complaint, for example, an "action agent" quickly assumes responsibility for resolving the matter. The action agent must respond quickly, since a "banner" message remains visible in the computer system until the problem is fixed.

Alfaro says the company learns new things every day as the result of the information gathered by ECHO—more than 1,200 comments each week. For example, the system enables USAA reps to be on the lookout for specific kinds of customer feedback, a capability that enables the company to carry on a kind of dialogue with its customers. Such customer feedback is then fed back inside the organization, acting as a kind of early warning system about things the company has to fix or about issues of concern to customers that the company needs to address, says Alfaro.

Creating an Information-Driven, Feedback-Engineered Organization

Alfaro believes that what he and others at USAA call "information-driven, feedback-engineered" organizations are the wave of the future. Corporate success in the next century, he says, will depend on a company's ability to leverage feedback and to generate an ongoing dialogue with customers as a result. This process will provide the basis for enduring customer relations based on trust and commitment. Technology, he says, is the "disciplinarian" that will enable this kind of service, speed, consistency, and accountability to be sustained for the long term.

USAA's sophisticated customer care and data-collection processes have helped propel the company to the top of its industry. Eighty-six percent of the company's inbound calls are successfully handled during the first contact. Sixty-nine percent of USAA's customers are in the top quintile for customer satisfaction. And 92 percent of USAA's customer base is in the top three quintiles of customer satisfaction. Small wonder, then, that USAA has an annual customer-renewal rate of 98 percent!

Mercedes-Benz: Partner for Life

Mercedes-Benz USA is another company that puts heavy emphasis on responsiveness and accountability to customers. "We aren't here just to sell you a car. We're here to be your partner and to meet all your automotive needs," says Bill Hurley, formerly the company's Manager of Customer Information and now Department Manager for New Media.

Like USAA, Mercedes-Benz' customer-service approach is predicated largely on the interaction that company phone reps have with customers, on the centralization of information at the fingertips of phone reps, and on systematic follow-through. These activities build corporate credibility and customer loyalty while enabling phone reps to react quickly when necessary and collect information that can be leveraged across the organization to serve different purposes.

Using sophisticated workstation technology, for example, Mercedes-Benz phone reps routinely develop highly detailed profiles of Mercedes-Benz customers; thus they typically know not only what car a customer owns, but also what cars that customer has owned in the past and whether a customer has just switched over from Jaguar.

Like USAA, Mercedes-Benz puts heavy stock on collecting "market intelligence" and customer feedback. Opinions about product quality and suggestions about product enhancements, for example, are routinely picked up from customer conversations and fed back to the company's North American marketing and manufacturing operations.

"Our customers like to talk with real people," notes Hurley. "We promote staying on the phone a long time with people." That intense customer contact is part of the company's goal of developing "cradle-to-grave" relationships with customers, he says.

Hurley likes to tell a story that illustrates just how quickly Mercedes-Benz can react to customer feedback and, in so doing, ingratiate itself in the minds of customers. One winter day a few years ago, he says, several owners of one particular model of Mercedes called in to complain of trouble starting their cars. Because Mercedes-Benz uses sophisticated technology to track call patterns and queries, the company soon realized that all the cars having problems had similar vehicle identification numbers. Within 24 hours, customer service reps had talked with German engineers and come up with a fix for the problem. Road-assistance crews were then dispatched to the homes and offices of Mercedes customers across the country to repair cars stuck in people's driveways and in company parking lots. The result? Mercedes-Benz scored a public relations coup and was perceived by customers as putting action behind its customer care philosophy.

Besides using technology to stay close to customers, Mercedes-Benz has made key organizational changes to help reinforce its customer care and marketing priorities. Outbound follow-up and promotions areas, formerly outsourced, have been brought in-house to ensure data integration and quality assurance. Since consolidation of its Customer Assistance Center, Mercedes-Benz' call-abandonment rates have fallen to 1 percent. Call volumes have increased because of improved service, and customer-satisfaction ratings continue to climb.

Sun MicroSystems: Delighting the Customer

Mercedes' approach to forging close ties with customers is also part of the customer care philosophy at Sun MicroSystems, a leading provider of hardware, software, and services to support corporate intranets and the Internet. Sun is focused on building and maintaining strong relationships with customers by responding to their needs and making it easy for them to do business with the company. In fact, the company's goal is to "delight its customers worldwide," says program manager MaryAnn Munroe.

Sun uses a combination of telesales and the Web to deliver sales and customer care services. Technology infrastructure and a suite of online tools enable Sun telesales personnel to integrate order entry and leads management functions with customer profiles and to access an online product catalogue that contains descriptions of some 5,000 products. Using these systems, telesales reps worldwide can access customer product histories and preferences and assist customers in the purchasing process. The systems can also show license requirements, systems requirements, and other information, says Munroe.

This data is especially helpful not only to answer inquiries relating to current products, but also to assist with upgrading sales or selling add-on service options to customers. "When we created our database structure, we did it in a way that would permit reps to talk to customers on the phone without having to go through files of data," says Munroe.

Because of extensive training, product knowledge, and use of online tools, Sun telesales reps can handle 99 percent of incoming customer queries in a single call. When necessary, they can also send e-mail messages directly from a customer's profile screen to product managers, who respond promptly to customer queries.

But Sun doesn't just offer customers a high-quality and responsive telesales organization. "More and more of our customers like the independence of using the Internet to place orders, check on order status, determine product availability, and get pricing information," says Munroe. She says that through Sun's online Sun-Store, customers can gain access to this and other information, although they can still call upon a phone rep if and when necessary as part of the transaction. "Our goal is to help customers do business with us in whatever way makes the most sense for them," Munroe says. "We think integrating phone and Internet capabilities is the very way to do that."

Chapter Conclusions

Companies like USAA, Mercedes-Benz, and Sun MicroSystems are all setting a new standard of customer care in business today. They're doing it by letting "service to customers" drive their organizational structure and by creating value-maximizing networks of technology, people, and processes that enable them to:

1. Respond with a speed, accountability, and responsiveness unmatched by their competitors

2. Engage in continuous product and process improvement

3. Pursue long-term information-driven competitive strategies that can position them for sustained marketplace success

4. Evolve organizationally as customer needs and marketplace requirements dictate.

From a strategic point of view, this last point is especially important. As noted at the beginning of this chapter, these companies don't fall into the trap of letting technological capability drive their business strategy. Instead, they view technology as a tool for supporting their business strategy (customer care) (see Figure 10.1).

This distinction is an important one. As we've noted elsewhere in this book, technology is a "transactional" change driver in the life of organizations, not a "transformational" driver. By itself, technology cannot effectively leverage the kind of change

Characteristic	Traditional Call Center ⇨	Advanced Call Center ⇨	Customer Care Network ⇨	Value- Maximizing Network
Degree of Integration	Functionally Isolated	Functionally Isolated	Among Customer Contact Units	Across the Enterprise
Company's Customer Care Philosophy	Just a Cost Center	Investment	Value Creator	Core Process
Emphasis	Productivity Reps	Customer Problem Resolution	Capturing & Sharing Knowledge About Customer	Leveraging Knowledge
Information Technology	• Paper-Intensive • Unintegrated Legacy Computer Systems • Extensive Wrap-up and Follow-up • Sharing is Incidental	• GUI Front Ends* • Customer Profile Databases • Sharing Interactions Within Company • Legacy Systems Not Integrated • Intelligent Call Routing	• Integration of Cross-Functional Legacy and Non-legacy Data • Real-Time Information • Collaborative Systems • Direct Customer Links	• Effective Aggregation, Analysis, and Dissemination of Information Across Enterprise • Information Used as the Basis for Developing Competitive Strategy

* GUI: Graphic User Interfaces

Figure 10.1 Where Technology and Strategy Work in Harmony

that's required to move a company in new business directions or sustain improvements in business performance. Transformational drivers—such as changes in culture, strategy, or leadership—are required for that, as USAA, Mercedes-Benz, and Sun MicroSystems all realize.

Companies like these have all framed technology choices, investments, and initiatives within a larger strategic change framework of providing superlative customer care—*the very nature of which is constantly evolving.* Doing this gives them organizational leverage to effectively differentiate themselves in their various marketplaces and to provide a level of service, reliability, and responsiveness to customers that their competitors can't touch.

Take a Long-Term Approach to Technology Planning

In an era of rapid technological change, planning the role that technology is to play in *your* organization is critical. Rapid deployment of new technologies often has a disruptive effect on organizational design, revenue streams, work flows, and employee productivity.

Decisions about technology, therefore, must never be made in a vacuum or witnout considering the human implications that their implementation will raise. Instead, IT decisions must be made in the context of a large-gauge organizational change framework that takes into account the possibility that customer needs may evolve, business goals may change, that a company may move in new strategic directions, or that organizational growth or business restructuring may put new demands on existing systems.

The failure to plan for such contingencies is one reason so many companies today are burdened by outdated legacy systems, which in too many cases act as a hindrance to business performance, not an enabler of it. Don't let your organization make this mistake.

Where is Your *Company on the Customer Care Continuum?*

Each of the companies that made our customer care "star" list is moving toward or has already created a value-maximizing network (VMN) in its organization. That's because each has dedicated itself to ensuring that everyone who needs to have the information has real-time access to it and to developing competitive strategies based on "market intelligence" gathered during ongoing contact with customers.

How can *you* move toward creating a value-maximizing network in your own company? Here are some guidelines for creating a customer care approach and strategy that will be profitable to your enterprise.

- **Understand the value of a customer.** Companies developing VMNs today carefully segment and target customers

continued

to ensure the profitability of a high-end customer care approach. They ask themselves questions such as, "What is the likely lifelong profitability of this particular customer?" Such targeting is essential to ensure effective expenditure of resources for marketing, sales, and other customer care activities.

- **Recondition your organization.** Networking your organization together (organizationally and technologically) is critical if you are going to create a value-maximizing network. You must, for example, knock down traditional "stovepipes" separating one part of the company from another and create "connective tissue" throughout the organization to facilitate the flow of information.

  How do you accomplish this? An organization's top leadership first must set the tone and create an organizational culture that stresses information-sharing. At the same time, senior and line managers must stress the importance of "continuously learning about the customer" as integral to the economic livelihood of the organization.

- **Move to optimize every customer contact.** Companies creating VMNs in today's business environment believe every customer contact creates value, both for the customer and the company. They view customers not through the "lens" of the next business transaction but in terms of their lifetime profitability.

- **Integrate information sources.** "Enabling technology" must effectively link the organization together electronically in ways that transcend organizational boundaries and the limitations of existing technology. Networking your organization facilitates the organization-wide sharing of information. It also ensures greater accountability and responsiveness in serving the needs of customers and assures an enhanced ability to deal with changing market conditions, that, if unaddressed, could adversely affect the business.

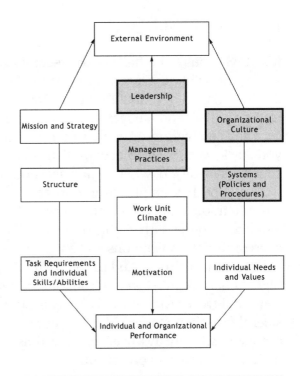

		External Environment		
		Leadership		Organizational Culture
Mission and Strategy		Management Practices		Systems (Policies and Procedures)
Structure		Work Unit Climate		
Task Requirements and Individual Skills/Abilities		Motivation		Individual Needs and Values
		Individual and Organizational Performance		

11 Beating the Millennium Bug: How the FAA Created a Culture of Commitment and Accountability to Solve the Y2K Problem

"When I talk to my colleagues in the private sector that work at Nike, for example, they have one goal: to make a profit and a great sneaker. In our case, we have a very large Board of Directors. Every member of Congress is a member of our Board. The National Transportation Safety Board is, as is the Inspector General. They all have different views of what our priorities should be, and staying focused on a single goal is a big challenge."

—Jane Garvey, FAA Administrator

It's 1998. You're the head of the federal agency responsible for ensuring the safety and security of America's skies, and you've got a deadline (January 1, 2000) for ensuring that all your computer, air traffic control, and navigation systems are Y2K compliant.

Besides having only a limited amount of time to complete your task, you have to accomplish it in a highly stovepiped and siloed organization, where quick decision-making, cross-functional work approaches, employee accountability, and information-sharing haven't traditionally been the norm. Making matters more challenging is the fact that you have to come up with a solution by overcoming the suspicions and enlisting assistance from those you regulate: the airlines. And to top it all off, you have to operate in a highly charged political environment, where everyone from politicians and the President to everyday air travelers and the press consider themselves stakeholders in your organization and where your agency hasn't always been perceived as able to complete critical high-profile projects on schedule.

How do you do it? If you're Federal Aviation Administration (FAA) Administrator Jane Garvey, the first conclusion you reach is that you've got to create a new culture of accountability and commitment inside your organization to ensure that the nation's air traffic control systems operate reliably through the year 2000 and beyond. To ensure that the management of Y2K renovation, repair, and conversion activities is a coordinated and organizationally disciplined effort, you create a special agency-wide Y2K Program Office to work across all lines of business in your organization. You appoint a strong director who enjoys punching holes in bureaucratic stovepipes to head this office, have him recruit a small but scrappy volunteer force from inside the agency to address "interoperability issues," "contingency planning," and other subjects critical to making the air traffic control system safe and reliable. Next, you make some strong pronouncements (e.g., "Aviation safety will not be compromised on January 1, 2000, or any other day"). Finally, you put stringent project benchmark dates in place, all the time communicating to your organization's 50,000 employees that "Y2K" is unlike any project they've ever been involved with before (or likely will be again) in terms of its importance to air travelers the world over.

That, in essence, is what Garvey, a former director of Boston's Logan Airport, did back in 1998 to ensure that the FAA's thousands of computers, navigational arrays, and air traffic control systems would be operating smoothly, safely, and efficiently come January 1, 2000. In doing so, she helped orchestrate a huge culture change in how the FAA has traditionally operated and created a new model of organizational problem-solving that may well be used to address other agency priorities in the future.

A Herculean Undertaking

By any stretch of the imagination, Garvey's task over the last two years has been gargantuan. As FAA Administrator, she has had to oversee the replacement or repair of some 430 "mission critical" systems that represent the very heart of America's air traffic control system.

Her job has required painstaking attention to issues such as contingency planning, resources planning, and allocation. And it has required huge amounts of coordination and cooperation between the FAA and other players in the aviation industry, including airlines, aircraft manufacturers, trade groups, vendors, and even foreign countries whose own civil aviation Y2K efforts are not controlled by the FAA.

Unique Challenges

With the year 2000 rapidly approaching, the Y2K challenges facing the FAA loomed large and had enormous implications. Unlike other organizations' Y2K problems, most of which required replacement or repair of individual computer systems, networks, or equipment, the FAA's challenges were exponentially more complex. America's air traffic control network consists of thousands of interconnected and interdependent systems, each of which must work flawlessly on its own and in tandem with others at all times. These systems are located across the United States and must work together to transmit data 24 hours a day, 7 days a week.

A Managerial Issue More than a Technical One

The possibility, however remote, that, come 2000, the nation's air traffic control system might blink or that a critical computer circuit might fail, causing planes to malfunction or air traffic controllers' screens to go dark, focused tremendous scrutiny on Garvey and the FAA beginning in the late 1990s. Despite that, however, Garvey has always maintained that "solving the Y2K problem is more a management and people issue than a technical issue" for the FAA.

Why is this the case? "I wouldn't for a minute downplay the technical challenges we've had with Y2K, but we have wonderful technicians who have undertaken modernization efforts in the past, if not necessarily at the pace that's been required with Y2K," she told us in a 1999 interview. "Y2K is a managerial issue for us because its successful completion has always boiled down to whether or not we could set the right milestones, the right deadlines, and ask the right questions to get to unknown problems."

Garvey adds that, when it comes to Y2K, the agency has done things right. It has asked itself the right questions and uncovered and addressed problems. But she acknowledges that the FAA hasn't *always* done a great job of managing large business projects on a timely or efficient basis, for several reasons:

First, the agency traditionally has taken a highly "stovepiped" approach to solving problems and managing projects, doing everything by individual lines of business and following a rigid command-and-control style of decision-making. Second, the agency has historically tried to do too many things at once. "In government, it is very easy to be pulled in 100 different directions at the same time," she told us. "When I arrived here as administrator, the FAA had nine strategic goals. You can't manage nine strategic goals and get anything done. You are just pulled too thin."

Finally, in the past, the agency had had a penchant for taking on projects that were either too massive or too ambitious. "We tended to take on large and complex projects, and, often, that meant we never got to the point of deployment," she says. "That's what happened here in the 1980s. At that time, we were trying to implement a very large modernization project, but it never got off the ground." As a result, the FAA acquired a reputation for less-than-stellar performance.

Keeping It Simple

For all these reasons, Garvey decided, shortly after becoming administrator in 1997, to scale the agency's goals down to just three, all of which focus around the themes of "safety, security, and system efficiency." And when the Y2K renovation and modernization imperative came along, she decided to frame Y2K goals in the context of these larger themes. She also mandated that Y2K issues be addressed on an organization-wide basis, with an agency-wide Y2K Program Office being responsible for establishing and maintaining "a structure, process, schedule, and milestones for Y2K repair efforts across the agency."

But Garvey realized that accomplishing these tasks and others that would be required for Y2K fixes to be implemented meant FAA employees had to take a new approach to their jobs. They'd have to become more accountable for results and work collaboratively across different lines of business. They'd have to practice risk-taking and out-of-the-box thinking to devise solutions to a "once in a century" problem. And there wasn't a whole lot of time to do any of this.

But these new approaches posed problems. FAA's culture was extremely layered and hierarchical. Power and decision-making were widely diffused throughout the organization. What's more, FAA's "slightly militaristic" culture—to use Garvey's words—tended to produce risk-averse employees. "Risk-taking is very difficult for bureaucrats," she says. "People are not rewarded for taking risks in government. Very often it's quite the opposite."

Sending a Signal about Y2K's Importance

So early in 1998, Garvey started emphasizing new approaches to solving the Y2K issue. She announced that it would become a key priority for the FAA, even at the expense of other projects. She put new performance agreements in place with senior managers, emphasizing Y2K compliance progress as a key performance metric. She placed the Y2K office just across the hall from her on the tenth floor of FAA headquarters, in Washington, D.C. She cut bureaucratic red tape so that decisions about Y2K issues could be made quickly and cleanly, without having to go through multiple layers of FAA management. She even brought in author and Y2K guru Peter de Jager, who told FAA employees that they shouldn't be afraid of failure but, rather, should look at failed attempts to make Y2K fixes as proof they were making progress.

All this was driven, of course, by the fact that Garvey and Ray Long, whom she had appointed Director of FAA's Y2K Program

Office in February 1998, didn't have the luxury of time to drive fundamental change inside the agency. The need to address Y2K compliance and interoperability issues was growing more and more critical every day, and Garvey and Long both knew they had their work cut out for them.

Everybody Was Doing Their Own Thing

"At the time of my appointment, there was no standard FAA-wide regimented approach to fixing the Y2K problem. Every line of business within FAA was doing its own thing," says Long. Thus, Long's office sprang into action to spearhead and coordinate Y2K repair and renovation efforts across the organization. One of the very first things it did was to select LOB (line of business) Y2K program managers. Other tasks included serving as an information and resource hub among the LOBs (including areas that oversaw the nation's air traffic control system and airports), monitoring and reporting the status of FAA Y2K activities, minimizing and managing the risks associated with the agency's Y2K efforts, and building links among people in the agency who'd never worked together before.

A Y2K Ambassador

Long himself became a kind of Y2K "ambassador," meeting and working closely with people from each line of business to ensure that they had the resources and help they needed. At the same time, the FAA embarked on a strategy of proactive industry outreach to airlines, airports, avionics manufacturers, telephone companies, and utilities by holding a series of "Industry Day" events. Designed to build trust and cooperative links among all segments of the aviation industry, these highly successful events helped create a spirit of cooperation and partnership around solving Y2K issues and identified areas of responsibility for Y2K fixes that different industry players would assume.

On top of all this, the agency set up communications links with manufacturers of critical airport systems, stressing the need for their products to be Y2K complaint. It also developed and distributed a comprehensive airport system checklist to more than 5,000 airports to help them identify and correct their own Y2K problems.

Proactive Industry Outreach

The unique nature of the Y2K problem was the chief driver behind such events and activities and the reason why building bridges among different segments of the aviation industry was so crucial. As Long notes, "It wasn't going to mean a lot if all of the FAA's systems were successively renovated and Y2K compliant in 2000 but there wasn't power to run them. As Y2K is a shared problem, events like 'Industry Days' and other activities have been important in working toward a shared solution."

Hiring a Y2K Program Team

But just as it wasn't easy for Garvey, as FAA Administrator, to drive Y2K readiness preparations from her office on the tenth floor of FAA headquarters, it wasn't easy for Long, as day-to-day manager of those activities, to operate, either. First, he had to build a staff to help him orchestrate Y2K compliance activities across a 50,000-person organization. He and his team had to help the organization take a painstaking series of five steps on the way to full Y2K compliance, beginning with a system-by-system assessment of systems to be repaired, followed by renovation and replacement of individual systems, troubleshooting of operations among scores of repaired or replaced computer platforms, and testing to be sure that the entire air traffic control system was free of bugs.

Long started the Y2K program office with a staff of just one person: himself. "After I was appointed, I sat in a cubicle by myself and said, 'Now what do I do?' " Shortly afterward, he began to recruit volunteers from all the FAA's lines of business to serve on his Y2K swat team, and, by the end of 1999, he had about 20 full-time FAA employees working on Y2K issues in his office. Along with an assortment of contractors and others working part time on the project in various FAA locations, Long estimates that no more than 150 or 200 people were ever dedicated to managing the project agency-wide at any given time. This may not sound like a big enough force to act as a catalyst for change in an organization, but Garvey and Long both say there were reasons to keep the Y2K team small.

"We kept the team relatively small because I was concerned that we not get too layered," says Garvey. She feared that, if it didn't remain small and agile, it could become as bureaucratic as other parts of the organization. "We also tried to bring in people with different strengths, to ensure we had the flexibility and skill depth we needed in managing things."

Long agrees. "We never put out a broadcast message and recruited 25 people at a time. Instead, we recruited one at a time because we wanted to find committed people who would put resolution of this problem above their own professional concerns."

What kind of people did Long hire for his team? In a mid-1999 interview, Long told us that he sought out people who, contrary to most people in the agency, would relish the opportunity to work in an unstructured environment, who would savor the opportunity to work on a project with huge implications for the future of the industry, and who might be looking for a sense of adventure, as well.

He knew they wouldn't be easy to find, but he knew these qualities would be essential as they tackled Y2K issues and tried to come up with system fixes. The very fact that the Y2K "problem" had never existed before meant there were no hard-and-fast rules to follow, no white three-ring binders to rely on in dealing with it. People would need to know how to improvise, ad-lib, stay focused on task, and mediate conflicts.

The specific answers Long gave to some of our interview questions reveals not only important insights into his style as a team leader, but also the challenges he and members of his team faced on a daily basis inside the FAA organization.

Your team is responsible for some key Y2K activities. It facilitates communication across FAA's different lines of business; it is involved in outreach efforts to industry groups. It's tasked to do many things. How do you know whom to pick for this kind of assignment?

Long: More than anything else, I'm looking for risk-takers, people who can move quickly, be problem-solvers, and be agile in handling the demands of this job because it's unique. So we've picked people carefully. We recruit one at a time, and we pick people we know or people we trust. They come here with the clear understanding that, if this doesn't work out, they'll have to go back to their own organization.

What makes the job unique?

Long: To solve this Y2K problem, we're breaking a lot of the old rules. We're forcing people to work together in ways they haven't done before. That means that everybody on this team has to be able to blast through barriers, ask hard questions of others, anticipate problems before they arise, and deal with all kinds of conflicts and questions. That can be grueling and grinding. So we've needed dedicated people who are committed to making our Y2K efforts succeed. We also need people to be strong self-starters. That's because around here we have no time for lessons learned. We don't have time to go out and do case studies. We don't have time to strategize and develop three-year strategic plans. In many cases, we're in a 'just do it' mode, and there's nobody you can go to and delegate problems to or blame when things go wrong. You have to be a problem-solver and, as I said before, a risk-taker by nature.

How do you turn people into risk-takers?

Long: I don't think you make people risk-takers. I think people are risk-takers by nature. I wouldn't jump out of an airplane with a parachute, even though you might convince me that it's going to open. I would never do it, but there might be people around me that would do that in a heartbeat.

   I know people that wouldn't take on this Y2K project, but they'd jump out of an airplane with a parachute. So the question we have to ask when we recruit people is whether or not they can take the kinds of risks required to be effective as members of our team.

Would you say, then, that what makes your team effective is making sure each member of the team is a good fit for the team's assignment?

Long: Absolutely. That's why we're an all-volunteer team. There's nobody in this office that's forced to be here. Nobody is permanently assigned to me. They're detailed, so from the moment they get here, they have to perform. We have lots to do. When we do recruit people, they're in here initially for 120 days. That gives me a chance to see if they're going to work out, and, if they do and seem to like it, then we keep them. Everybody who is on the team right now is here for the duration. In two years, we've only lost two people who didn't feel like this was for them.

What qualities do you look for when you recruit team members?

Long: Well, besides being able to take risks, I look for people who can communicate honestly and in a forthright way. We're dealing with a project that has rigid deadlines associated with it, so every team member needs to communicate honestly and on a timely basis with everybody else.

They also have to be very results-oriented. In the past, the FAA often had a reputation for letting due dates on projects slip. In some cases, major aerospace projects were delayed by months or even years! We don't have that luxury here. With this project, it isn't what you don't know that will burn you; it's what you don't know you don't know. So our team philosophy is, 'Don't tell me something in July that I should have known last April.' We don't have that kind of time.

To make sure we don't run into unanticipated problems, we do 60-day reviews. Every 60 days, we look at what we've been working on and where the problems have been. We look at what's worked and what hasn't. We talk about the things that aren't working. We don't hide them. We don't play games. In fact, we don't allow anybody in this group not to be open about where we are with things.

What other traits do team members need to possess?

Long: I want people who are innovative thinkers. That's because what we're doing here—troubleshooting problems and brainstorming solutions—requires creative thinking. So as I said, people need to be problem-solvers. I don't have the answers to all the problems and challenges that come up, and, because of that, I don't let people delegate work up to me. Nobody in my office is allowed to come in and let me make all the decisions.

Given that the work environment you've created inside the Y2K program team is quite different from the prevailing culture in the FAA as a whole, how do you effectively manage and motivate people to perform to your expectations?

Long: Well, that's interesting. You've heard all those jokes about federal government employees, that they don't work that hard and that they're only concerned about job security and where their next job will be. I couldn't disagree with that more intensely. The people we've recruited to be part of our team are highly dedicated to making our efforts succeed. In essence, we've made good matches.

I've seen people put in lots of 12- and 16-hour days on this project. I've seen people here in our Y2K Program Office on Saturdays, working to resolve issues. They don't claim any overtime. They're in this to win. And that makes me very proud of them.

In many cases, the best way I can motivate people to perform is to simply get out of the way. I want people to succeed and excel. And one of the beauties of working on this Y2K team is that a lot of what we're doing has not been done before. So we need people's passion, emotions, and imaginations working every day. Instead of this job being about people filling job boxes on an organization chart, it's about people using their imaginations to come up with creative solutions. I often tell people, for example, that we have to do more than simply make it to the playoffs—we've got to win the Super Bowl. I'm a results-oriented manager, and I expect to see people make progress, not excuses. There's no time here for people to think just about themselves or to complain.

Do you take time to celebrate 'small successes' along the path to full completion of the project?

Long: We don't do as much of that as we should. Again, because we don't have much time. But it's very important that we do pause, from time to time, to remember that each of us is a human being. And I'll say this: We maybe don't celebrate our successes as much as we should, but this is the tightest group of people I've ever had the privilege to work with.

Why do you think it's so tight?

Long: Because we've got a really important job to do. And we're going to be leaving our fingerprints on the fixes that we come up with, so we want to do our best. The bar is high, but I think that energizes people, and I know it has helped to energize other people in this organization, as well. I think everybody on this team wants one day to look back on their involvement here as being a pivotal time in their career, a time when they really had a chance to grow, stretch themselves, and learn.

What do you want the history of this team's work to be, once the Y2K project is complete?

Long: Our real challenge here is to use everything we're doing as an organizational learning experience. We can't allow these fixes, or the work we've done in bringing the LOBs together to solve problems, or the best practices we're developing as we go forward to simply evaporate and not be used again. We have to build what we've learned how to do into the FAA organizational culture, to make it better and more functional than it's been. In fact, I look upon that as the sixth and final phase of our Y2K repair and renovation efforts. It's the work we'll do after the click of the calendar in January 2000.

Routing the Millennium Bug

As of this writing, it is not yet the year 2000, so the final Y2K fixes that Long and his Y2K team helped to make by working with their FAA co-workers have yet to be fully tested. But this much is certain. As Y2K renovation and repair efforts proceeded through both 1998 and 1999, Long saw a curious thing happen. Just as his team began to coalesce around solving Y2K problems, a similar thing started to occur in the FAA employee population as a whole. In many cases, people who had never worked together before were thrust together, usually at the instigation of or with the help of Long's team, to come up with fixes relating to everything from computer interfaces to network interoperability. And as time went by, people began to get on the bandwagon. Long, for example, recalls one instance in which engineers at the FAA's Atlantic City technical center were busy testing data links as part of the validation phase of the FAA's Y2K preparation activities.

A New Culture of Collaboration

"When I went to our technical center in New Jersey, I witnessed live testing of our traffic control system, a critical test of just how well our software and computer systems would operate," he says. "But the most significant thing I witnessed was 75 people who had never worked together before holding hands, high-fiving one another saying, 'We did it. We pulled this off!' That was unusual. There are two or three different organizations at the technical center, and each has a different boss. Nonetheless, they all worked together to make this happen. It was emotional for them. They reached out to work with the National Weather Service, the Canadians, and our MCI telecommunications facility in Richardson, Texas. I wouldn't have seen that kind of collaboration and team effort among people in the past."

More and More People Taking Ownership

Another example of how people came together to resolve Y2K issues became evident in the weekly meetings that Long and his team members held with program managers from each of the FAA's seven lines of business. "When we started a couple of years ago, we were very dysfunctional. People came together in our Y2K Command Center once a week, but nobody wanted to talk to anybody else. We didn't share ideas. We didn't feed off each others' successes and failures. By the end of the project, however, we saw an entirely different dynamic in those meetings. People shared what they knew with one another. They helped each other. We saw it with the associate administrators, too, as they took personal ownership of Y2K issues, which, of course, is key. You have to get people to take ownership for what's happening. If you don't, you're dead."

The team efforts that Long saw emerge, both within his program team staff and in the larger FAA employee population, helped the organization meet a whole schedule of critical Y2K benchmark dates and testing deadlines leading up to the very end of 1999. Garvey gives credit for this to FAA's employees, of course, but especially to Long and members of his team, who she feels played an essential role in telegraphing the urgency of change throughout the FAA and in helping people get focused on the urgency of solving the Y2K problem at an operational level.

"In large bureaucracies, you often find that responsibilities are dispersed, so it's hard to appoint or select a single person or team that will be responsible for meeting a project's objectives," she says. "In our case, with Ray Long's team spearheading day-to-day management of Y2K efforts, we pulled it off by setting clear milestones and benchmarks and making it clear that we had to meet these no matter what. Ray also deserves credit for identifying people within FAA's various lines of business who have come together to solve this issue."

Chapter Conclusions

What are the lessons about organizational change that emerge from the FAA's experience in addressing Y2K issues? Clearly, the FAA has learned how to take an agency-wide approach in tackling a major organizational issue and, in so doing, has helped lay the foundation for a new, more responsive, and more efficient organizational culture. As this chapter reveals, a fundamental shift in people's work styles and behaviors began to occur as Garvey stressed the urgency of addressing the Y2K issue and as Long made it clear to his team members what work behaviors and attitudes would be required of them.

Creating a Culture of Alignment

In the FAA's case, the development of a new culture—in this case, one of greater internal alignment and accountability—will clearly be critical to the future work of the agency. Notes Garvey: "Today we're finding that almost every initiative we undertake really runs across all lines of business within this organization."

Garvey points to two projects beyond Y2K that will require a strong and focused agency-wide approach to implement. One of these, digital display replacement (DDR), involves the updating of computer screens that controllers use to track and plot the routes of airplanes in the air. The other, Free Flight Phase One, represents, in essence "the next generation in air traffic control." It will provide air traffic controllers with new advanced automation tools for determining air traffic schedules and routes farther in advance, thereby helping airlines optimize use of fuel and airplanes.

Another thing revealed in this chapter, as in others, is the essential role strong leadership plays in creating the "environmental conditions" for change to occur. Garvey's efforts early in 1998 to align performance metrics and articulate the urgency of resolving Y2K issues created a "climate of alignment" to support and sustain the agency's Y2K efforts for the long haul.

Staying Focused Was Key to Success

One of Garvey's principal challenges, however, was to keep the agency focused on its Y2K goals, not easy to do in any case but especially not under the spotlight of public scrutiny. "When I talk to my colleagues in the private sector that work at Nike, for example.

They have a single goal: to make a profit *and* a great sneaker," Garvey notes. "In our case, we have a very large Board of Directors. Every member of Congress is a member of our Board. The National Transportation Safety Board is, as is the Inspector General. They all have different views of what our priorities should be. So staying focused on a single goal is a big challenge."

Teams Are Critical at the Operational Level

Another lesson that emerges from this chapter is the vital role teams play in driving change efforts at an operational level in organizations. Long's Y2K program team clearly played a catalytic role in helping to integrate the FAA's Y2K efforts across all LOBs. Team members functioned in multiple ways: as facilitators, planners, coordinators, and communicators, bringing people together who, in many cases, had never worked together before.

Still other learnings emerge from this chapter that have special implications if one is considering a systems implementation or technology upgrade in an organization. The following suggestions go beyond the realm of Y2K efforts and apply to any organization-wide technology initiative. To ensure optimal success:

- **Make sure your organization's top leader is clearly seen as an active catalyst for change**. He or she must be visibly and vigorously behind deployment of the technology, as Jane Garvey and Ray Long were at FAA.

- **Position the introduction of systems implementations or technology upgrades as transformation initiatives critical to the future productivity and efficiency of the organization.** This emphasis creates a sense of urgency around the project.

- **Consider a dramatic leadership move to emphasize that you are serious about change.** Many of today's most effective change leaders say that one of the best ways to accelerate change initiatives is to temporarily reassign senior managers to dedicated positions surrounding such projects. This move sends the message to employees that an organization is truly serious about the changes it is implementing. In the FAA's case, Garvey took Long out of his job with the air traffic control section (where he was spearheading Y2K efforts) to head up efforts agency-wide.

- **Use every conceivable in-house communications channel to convey information about the systems implementation to employees of your organization and to make sure the messages you send employees are clear, consistent, frequent, and "multichannel."** Too many change makers take communications for granted or assume that, once a project has been launched, they need do nothing else to sell it to employees. Organizational entropy, employee indifference, and project overload sometimes causes system implementations to fail or get derailed. For that reason, keep communicating with employees about what is expected of them as system implementation efforts proceed.

- **Link the implementation of any new system to simultaneous human resources initiatives to reinforce the importance of new ways of working.** A good way to ensure success with new technology or systems is to link their introduction with new management practices, new job descriptions, updated training programs, and employee coaching and mentoring efforts. Doing so helps change work attitudes, habits, and behaviors, and ultimately leads to a new work culture.

- **Celebrate small victories on the way to full and successful system implementation.** Orchestrating any kind of organizational change is tough. It wears people out, frequently demoralizing them in the process. One reason is that, many times, people develop awareness of what needs to change before their organization has the means to fully bring it about. Their frustration may appear to be rebellion against (or resistance to) change, but it is, in fact, frustration over not being able to change as quickly as needed. For this reason, rewarding and acknowledging people for hard work is often more important to their continued morale and motivation than are cash rewards or other financial compensation. As Garvey noted in our interview with her, "Let people know that you appreciate what they are doing. Often people aren't looking for pay increases. They want recognition that their work is valued, that their contribution is appreciated, and that they are making a difference to the success of their organization."

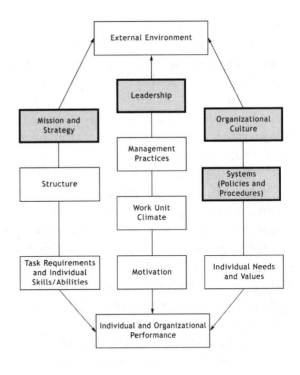

	External Environment	
	Leadership	
Mission and Strategy		Organizational Culture
	Management Practices	
Structure		Systems (Policies and Procedures)
	Work Unit Climate	
Task Requirements and Individual Skills/Abilities	Motivation	Individual Needs and Values
	Individual and Organizational Performance	

12 The Case for Charismatic Leadership: Why Former NatWest Bancorp EVP Roger O. Goldman Banks on the Power of Personality to Help Drive Change

"When a leader enters deeply into enemy territory with the troops, he brings out their potential. He has them burn the boats and destroy the pots, none knowing where they are going."

"To assemble armies and put them into dangerous situations is the business of generals."

—Sun Tzu, *The Art of War*

As you ponder the best way to manage change in your organization, what elements will be most important to consider? We've noted that strong executive leadership is typically the chief engine of change in companies, especially at the beginning, but what *kind* of leadership does your organization need: quiet and consistent, or colorful and charismatic?

Elsewhere in this book, we profile examples of strong and steady CEOs who, more often than not, provided quiet examples of executive leadership, who nudged their organizations along, and who were successful primarily because they provided stability and continuity, even in the midst of change. But what of the charismatic leader, the person who leads as much by style and force of personality as by vision and strategy? Some business pundits contend that *charismatic* leaders are the only kind who count when it comes to managing successful change.

Others argue that the innate narcissism of some charismatic CEOs (e.g., Sunbeam's former CEO, "Chainsaw Al" Dunlap) can be destructive and distracting when it creates a cult of personality around a single individual, results in absurdly huge CEO compensation packages, or fosters the belief that most organizational problems can be solved if you simply rule by fear and intimidation.

In our view, there are times when charismatic leadership is exactly what a company needs, such as when a company is in a performance slump, when visionary leadership has long been lacking, or when it's critical to reenergize employees who have grown weary and shell-shocked from year after year of downsizing and restructuring. As a charismatic leader, Roger O. Goldman has had to deal with all these scenarios—and in one of the most change-resistant of all industries: banking.

As the former Executive Vice President of National Westminster Bancorp (NatWest) and Group Head of the bank's Community Banking Group from 1991 to 1996, Goldman oversaw an operation that served nearly a million consumer and small and medium-sized businesses in the New York City metropolitan area. During this time, Goldman helped stop the bank's financial hemorrhaging and transformed it into an engine of steady business growth, a feat he accomplished by creating 800 separate profit centers within the bank and pushing authority and responsibility as far down in the organization as possible.

With an unruly mane of salt-and-pepper hair, a flair for expressive phrases (he likes to pop "Rogerisms" at anyone who enters his office), and a tough Jimmy Breslin-like demeanor that strikes you as straight off the streets of New York, Goldman is a self-described charismatic leader in an industry where top executives can be indistinguishable suits, colorless and bland rather than pugnacious and bold. He enthusiastically claims credit for introducing the most successful sales campaign ever in NatWest's history, and for dramatically increasing the bank's reputation for customer service. By his own admission, however, Goldman's success at NatWest was due less to his managing things "by the numbers" and more to his ability to create a vision of a successful business, to size people up, and to motivate them to make that vision real.

We caught up with Goldman in his offices in New York City, where today he serves as President of Global Sourcing Services, a major direct marketing and outsourcing company. We spoke with him about his leadership style, how he has used change-readiness assessments to guide his own actions as a leader, and what he has learned about himself and about managing people in the course of a 20-year career in banking and financial services.

Roger, when you went to NatWest, you had to make tough decisions very quickly about how you'd make the bank more competitive and profitable. How do you size people up to determine who will support you in driving change and who will resist you?

Goldman: In any organization, you have four types of people. Two percent of the people are sycophants. They're the ones who, when you're new to the job, walk in and say, 'Thank God you're here.' You probably ought to fire those people when you hear that because that's probably what they said to the guy you replaced. There are about a third of the people, who, as soon as you start creating a new vision for the organization, sign right up for it. Another third say, 'Hey, this is interesting, but I need more information,' and a third who say, 'Screw you! I'm not gonna do that!'

My advice is: Don't worry about the people who immediately sign up with you. You've got *them*. They'll support you in any kind of change effort. And don't worry about the people who say 'screw you,' 'cause they're already gone. What you've got to do is focus on the people in the middle who are looking for more information, for inspiration. Help them to expand their comfort zone with what you're doing, and they'll ally themselves with the already convinced.

You went to NatWest Bank at a time when it was having signifi-cant financial problems. How do you get large groups of people to follow you? You can't possibly spend enough one-on-one time with everybody to make personal connections with them, can you?

Goldman: I am a charismatic leader. I connect with people through my personal style. One of the things I'm good at is creating a vision that makes sense for people and then getting people to sign up for it. That's arrogant to say, of course, but I think it's true. It's worked for me in the past. In my experience, everybody likes to win, and I'm able to show them how.

I spent a long time in my career trying to find extraordinary people to hire and work with. Then I realized that was dumb. If you're managing mass, you have to create an environment where ordinary people become capable of extraordinary things. It begins by making people a little uncomfortable with where they are and helping them realize what they're capable of achieving. You also have to give them some structure because most people in business nowadays don't trust their intuition.

To create that structure at NatWest, you used an organizational as-sessment instrument to determine what you had to change, correct?

Goldman: That's right. FDR once said, 'Nobody leads. People fol-low, and the essence of leadership is making sure your followers are there.' So I used the Burke-Litwin change-readiness assessment instrument as an analytic tool to help me and my organization un-derstand where our followers (our employees) were.

At the time, we were trying to become a more market-driven organization. The assessment helped us to understand the discon-nect that existed between what our people were thinking and what we needed them to do if we were to become more competitive in the marketplace. We did the assessment on two occasions, about 18 months apart. The first time we did it, we learned that most people didn't understand where we were going and didn't know what they were supposed to do to help us be successful. They needed more direction. I mean the disconnect was huge. Reading the assessment's findings clued me in to the need to go out and communicate to people about what kind of bank we were aiming to be. So I got off my butt and did that.

I went on the road for a year to explain my vision of the bank to over 5,000 people in 800 profit centers and support offices. I did this to get people's support and to explain what we needed them to do if we were to be successful. In our case, it was about serving customers, communities, and our fellow employees. 'Everybody has to be part of this effort. Everybody has to give 110 percent,' I told employees. 'We're going to reinvent peoples' jobs and hold everybody more accountable for results.'

After a year and a half of doing that, we did another assessment. This time we found out that, while people now knew where we were going, they didn't feel they were being properly supported by IT, reward systems, and other things. And though I was depressed at the time with that finding, I realized later that we'd made progress because people had now made the connection between mission and strategy and how their individual jobs related to both. It caused us to shift our focus at that point and begin doing things at a 'transactional' level to help people do their jobs better and be more accountable for the jobs they were doing.

What specifically did you do?

Goldman: One thing we did was to decentralize the bank and create a franchise operation where small groups of people, generally eight to ten, were responsible for generating profits. The idea for doing this comes right out of group theory. Basically, you create an ideal group size where everyone can relate to each other, then you hold people accountable to some very basic metrics, which, of course, in a bank, is essential. This became our business model, and it worked. We used it in bank branches, our credit-card operation, and in our home-mortgage offices.

You then undertook a big sales campaign to reinforce the importance of employees working in a different way with customers, right?

Goldman: Right. I had some aggressive business targets I had to reach. To do that, we needed to get sales prospects into branches, and we needed people in the branches to sell more products and services. But I didn't position this with employees as a sales campaign because I knew people didn't want to be asked to do *that.* Instead, I told people to invite customers in for 20- or 30-minute chats so they could get to know them better, find out the names of their kids, get an idea about what their goals and dreams for the future were, things like that. The reps recorded all this stuff on a form.

What happened is that, as reps had these conversations with customers and got to know them as people rather than 'prospects,' they began selling new products and services to them. It was all reverse psychology. Reps sold stuff almost in spite of themselves. And they started coming up to me to tell me how much stuff they were selling to customers. We pulled 350,000 sales prospects into our branches this way. During the three years we were engaged in this marketing campaign, we dramatically increased our revenues per customer. We increased our market share and pretax profits, too—all without benefit of acquisition. And all in a *stagnant* market!

From that campaign, I learned that, to be an effective leader and to influence a big audience of people to do something you want them to do, you have to get out of your own head and into theirs. You have to demand that people use good judgment and common sense, things people are very capable of but often aren't asked to use! You also have to treat people as adults. For example, we gave branch managers the power and money to set business hours to fit their geographic market and clientele. Our branches were open at 7:30 A.M. in some places and stayed open in others until 9 P.M.

As this sales campaign was going on, you were traveling around to NatWest branches. How did you get people fired up?
Goldman: Well, first of all, I didn't spend a lot of time talking to people about the business or even about numbers. Instead, I went around and asked people questions like, 'Are you happy here?' 'Are you doing something you want to be doing?' 'What do you want on your tombstone?' 'Are you doing things to help you achieve that?' 'Are you living a life that is going to take you in that direction?'

My goal in doing this was to focus on *them,* on what they wanted and had identified as their own goals. It was a way to build alignment with what NatWest was doing. We also beefed up our systems support, provided people with better computers, software, and such.

My psychology with all this was subtle, but it was also relentless. As I said before, I believe that if you want people to change (in our case, they had to become more sales and customer oriented), you have to make them uncomfortable with the status quo, with where they are. You have to reach into their guts and give them a chance to actualize and achieve new things. This is what gets people engaged with me. It's brag, of course, but it works. I've influenced a lot of people's lives for the better because of the way I talk to them. In the course of this campaign, I helped a lot of people become more productive in their jobs, become more effective with customers, sell more stuff—even though they didn't realize they were doing it—and improve our bottom line as a result.

One of your employees felt so inspired by the way you talked to her that she opted to leave banking, didn't she?

Goldman: That's true. And that, too, taught me a lot about my effect on other people. One day I was at a bank branch in Long Beach Island, New Jersey, and a manager came up to me and said she was quitting. She explained that she'd been with the bank for 25 years and had joined it as an unwed mother at 17. Over the years, she'd been promoted many times but never felt worthy of any of her promotions, so she kept working at her job, year after year, getting heavier and heavier, because she didn't feel worthy of the good things that were happening to her. Then, after hearing me give a talk one day about goals, she concluded she was entitled to happiness after all. She realized she wasn't really where she wanted to be and decided to leave the bank to pursue a career in the Methodist ministry along with her son, which she was really excited about. She even managed to talk the seminary into giving her a full scholarship for it. She told me about all this and was ecstatic.

Now, mind you, this is a woman I'd never spent any one-on-one time with! Yet somehow I helped change her life. By the time she finished telling me her story, she was crying, and I was crying. Looking back on that experience, it was probably the best 15 minutes I had with NatWest in five years because I helped this woman identify what was important to *her*. Now, obviously, most people I talked with didn't leave the bank. But my point is, I reached something deep, deep inside her, and it resulted in a dramatic change.

What else did you learn from that experience?

Goldman: Not only that I can touch people and help make a difference in their lives, but that, if you want people to change, you have to show them what's in it for them. You know, at one time in my life I thought about becoming a shrink. That was 20 years ago. I went and talked to a bunch of shrinks, though, and they all asked me, 'How many people do you think you influence in a year?' And I said, 'Maybe 50,' which was the number of people who reported to me at the time. And every one of them said to me, 'Well, hell, we're lucky if we help half that number of people make changes.'

It was then that I decided being a business executive was a great vehicle for changing the world. Being a charismatic leader means helping other people have a larger vision of what they can achieve for themselves. If you can do that, you'll help your company grow bigger and get more profitable as a result. You'll help people live better lives, and maybe, just maybe, you'll change the world.

You sound like a guy with a big heart. Is that true?

Goldman: Yeah, I guess. But people shouldn't be deceived. In times of change, you have to be absolutely ruthless with people who don't get off their butts to work. Especially when there's a business agenda to attend to. One of my favorite sayings about business is this: 'We're in a war: We carry the wounded; we shoot the stragglers.' What I mean by that is that I'll help anybody that wants to come with me. But I'm not going to abide anybody who idles, especially if a company has to change in order to survive. Business *is* war, and you've got to be ruthless about pursuing it.

So is managing change a kind of military campaign?

Goldman: Oh, yeah. As a change leader, you need to be a general. You have to have vision and intuition to lead your troops successfully; you need to inspire them to act, but also be tough as nails on those who try to hold you back. You have to plan and be prepared, but you can't wait too long to act. And sometimes you've got to both push and pull people to go forward while you prepare their minds for the battle ahead. It's all part of getting the very best from people that you can, which is what gives you the margin of success in *any* military campaign.

But managing change is also about growing flowers. Really! I like to think of the organizations I've transformed as being like gardens. In any garden, you plant a lot of flowers, water them, protect them, nurture them, and let them grow. They won't always grow the way you hope they will, and not all of them will make it. But, over time, if you do all the right things to nurture flowers, you'll wind up with a beautiful garden.

You obviously believe in the power of charismatic leadership as a way to galvanize and unite people. Are their downsides to it in your mind?

Goldman: Oh, yeah! For one thing, you get fired 80 percent of the time because charismatic leadership scares people. Remember MacArthur? He got his walking papers. So you have to know when and if charismatic leadership is the style of leadership that's likely to be accepted by headquarters. That was something that neither MacArthur, or Patton, for that matter, ever paid much attention to.

So a charismatic leader has to pick his or her battles carefully, right?

Goldman: Definitely. As a charismatic leader, you have to make sure when to be out there leading the cavalry and when to be a team player. You have to have a good sense of timing because there are times when you can proceed on your own and times when you need to get 'permission' from outside stakeholders for what you're doing—from an external board of directors, for example, or employee groups.

Okay, so what do external stakeholders need to know if they're planning on hiring a charismatic leader, be it to turn a company around or energize employees to perform to new levels?

Goldman: First off, charismatic leaders make mistakes. It's inevitable. In fact, it's a sign you're being successful, just like it is with ballplayers. In baseball, if you screw up seven out of ten times at bat, you get into the Hall of Fame. The notion of being a good hitter in baseball isn't to keep the bat on your shoulder (do that, and you'll never get a hit). It's not to swing at too many bad pitches, either. What you've got to do is swing when it seems appropriate. You've got to rely on your instinct, skill, and experience. And, of course, you've got to keep your eyes on the ball.

The same things hold true for charismatic leaders, if they are to be successful. You've got to take some risks and encourage others to take risks, too. And because making mistakes is inevitable when you're managing change, you've got to create enough tolerance in your organization for people to do just that—to fail once in a while and hopefully fast, so that everybody learns from the experience. Fail to fail once in a while, and you'll ultimately fail to succeed.

There's something else, too. To be an effective leader, no matter what kind you are, requires you to have had at least one significant failure in your own life. Because your philosophy about life, about managing people, about running a company doesn't count for much if you haven't been punched to the mat a few times.

What else do you need to be an effective charismatic leader?

Goldman: A charismatic leader has to sell, not tell. He has to convince people that where he's trying to take a business makes sense for them. It also helps if you can surround yourself with smart people who are good with details. For example, I just hired two guys from the Stanford tennis team to handle some big client projects for me. Both of them are dynamite with spreadsheets and good with analytical thinking. A charismatic leader needs people like that around him, people who aren't afraid to challenge him occasionally but who'll also let him operate at an instinctual or gut level most of the time.

One last thing: As a charismatic leader, do you have a slogan, a favorite aphorism that captures the essence of what you think leadership is all about?

Goldman: As a matter of fact, I do. I first saw it hanging on the wall in my kid's second-grade class. It comes from one of the Star Wars movies, where Yoda is training Luke Skywalker to be a Jedi Knight, and Yoda says to Skywalker, 'There's no try. Only DO!' That sums up my business philosophy in a heartbeat. To be an effective change maker, you don't try. You *do.* And you keep doing it until you succeed. As a business leader, you often don't have the luxury to *try* things; you've got to act and achieve results. You plan, of course. You improvise. But, at times, you have to ad-lib as well, especially when you and your organization are learning what's involved in really managing change. Managing change is a process, not an event. There are always bumps in the road, but they don't have to rattle you. What you need to do in those cases is simply keep pushing on.

Chapter Conclusions

As you can see from this chapter, Roger Goldman is, to say the least, an iconoclastic leader who wears his heart on his sleeve and who expects a lot of the people he leads. While his leadership style wouldn't fit every company, he and other charismatic leaders like him bring to their organizations the kind of heartfelt enthusiasm and energy that is too often lacking in organizations and workplaces today and which is sometimes the critical deciding factor in whether an organization succeeds or not. Imagine, for example, the United States getting out of the Depression without Franklin D. Roosevelt to inspire us to new heights. Or England surviving the Battle of Britain without Churchill broadcasting from his hardened bunker that it was, indeed, England's "finest hour."

The Power of Personality

In regards to charisma, Goldman is an interesting contrast to Colin Marshall of British Airways (see Chapter 6), yet what the two leaders clearly have in common is persistence. In their respective change efforts, they "stayed the course," bounced back from mistakes, dealt with resistance, and kept people focused on the mission and strategy.

It's interesting to note that, as a leader, Goldman wants the whole person involved in his organization, not merely a nonfeeling, uncaring robot who does no more than what is minimally required of the job. He wants people to enjoy their work and to share the passion for it as he does. In this respect, Goldman is not unlike Herb Kelleher of Southwest Airlines. Both these leaders are role models for their people in that they bring their whole persons to their jobs.

It can be said of Goldman that he doesn't exactly suffer fools gladly. More important for leadership is the desire on his part to have no sycophants, no "yes" people around him. The successful leader welcomes challenges from followers, and, as Warren Bennis has stressed, the followers' main responsibility is to tell the boss the *truth*. Without truthful information, a leader will eventually fail. It's just a matter of time. The buck may stop at the leader's desk, but the leader must know what color the buck is, how big it is, what it feels and smells like, and so forth.

A further gift of Goldman's and what every leader should strive to obtain is the ability to make highly complex organizational and business matters simple and straightforward. His sales campaign is a beautiful example of this.

Finally, it would be hard to question the fact that Goldman is a leader. At the same time, however, he is a man of the people. Again, like Marshall of BA, he rarely sat in his office and pushed paper. He was constantly out and about at NatWest talking to people and asking questions, not just about the business but also about employees as human beings. Successful leaders mingle, they touch people's lives, and they show that they are human, too.

PART THREE

Epilogue

THE FUTURE OF CHANGE

As we said at the beginning of this book, we're living in a time of rapid and revolutionary change. The confluence of social, techno-logical, economic, marketplace, and political forces in the world today is not only rapidly reshaping the business landscape but also affecting the nature of society and the world community.

The transformation stories we've shared in this book provide you with snapshots of how numerous companies and organizations are managing successful transformation efforts today. The inter-views provide insights into the thinking and plans of some of today's top transformational leaders as they deal with sea changes in their respective industries and markets. And the model for managing change that we presented in Chapter 2 is designed as a template that can be used to grasp the dynamics of growth and performance in organizations and create change roadmaps.

So what does the future hold for *your* company?

The Future Promises More of the Same: Discontinuous Change

We stated in Chapter 1 that Moore's Law is a metaphor for the kind of change taking place in the business environment today. Change is no longer linear or incremental. It is rapid, discontinuous, and exponential—both in nature and impact. Among our predictions for the future:

- Marketplace turbulence will persist (especially in emerging economies), and "phase shifts" are likely to accelerate.

- Continued introduction of new information technologies (IT) will initially have disruptive effects on companies' organizational design until they are aligned and integrated to support business strategies.

- Industry and marketplace convergence will continue, speeded by the further emergence of the Internet and the growth of e-business.

- Continuing technical and manufacturing breakthroughs are likely to lead to vastly improved infrastructures inside companies, helping them to sustain increased productivity and operating efficiencies.

Finally:

- The pace at which new scientific discoveries are made is likely to mirror the dynamics of Moore's Law, with new knowledge doubling on a regular basis.

An interesting example of what's happening in the scientific realm can be seen by looking at the field of genomics research, which identifies genes and different gene combinations used in everything from new drugs to engineered foods. Monsanto Co. says its costs for determining the amino acid sequences that make up a gene—the basic building block of life—have dropped from $2.5 million in 1974 to just $150 today! As a result, Monsanto says its library of genetic information and the databases of all other major drug and agricultural companies in the biotechnology field are doubling every 12 to 24 months.[1]

Developments such as those we've just outlined suggest exciting business opportunities for tomorrow's companies—and tomorrow's workers. Nonetheless, challenges of "adaptation" await companies in virtually all industries as the twenty-first century begins. Among them:

The emergence of e-business will accelerate the organizational redesign of companies. This change will require companies to become even more agile and organizationally committed to change than they are today. The growth of the World Wide Web, for example, is rapidly generating new models of organizational design and business transactions. *The New York Times* reported in a March 22, 1999, story that 1999 may well go down as the "Year of the Affiliate," as Web merchants realize that one way to generate profits is to recruit other Internet sites to help sell their goods. The article points out that companies such as Amazon.com have been widely credited with pioneering the affiliate model of business.

But it isn't just Web-based upstarts or high-tech companies that are getting into the act today. The *Times* reports that today's electronic commerce partnerships "range from deals between companies with established brands to arrangements that retailers make with individuals who have built personal home pages."[2] Given the explosive growth in electronic commerce today, your company had better be braced to deal with the implications it will have for your relationships with customers, suppliers, and even competitors. Why? Because as Microsoft Chairman Bill Gates notes, the twenty-first century will belong to those who live and breathe a "Web lifestyle."

More and more companies will develop "customer care" strategies and use them as competitive differentiators. This change is part of a growing business trend that favors delivering "high value" over "high volume." This strategy is being adopted by a growing number of companies today "because customers are willing to pay a premium for goods and services that exactly meet their needs and because [a] high-value business cannot easily be duplicated by high-volume competition around the world," notes economist Robert Reich.[3] As we saw in Chapter 10, companies like USAA, Mercedes-Benz, and Sun MicroSystems have already adopted this kind of strategy. We predict still more companies will go this route in the future, given the high cost of acquiring new customers, business overcapacity in many industries, and strong Wall Street pressures to sustain longer-term profit pictures.

Many knowledge companies will develop and implement strategies for managing high employee growth. A 1999

PricewaterhouseCoopers' study by Pam Weber found that a variety of companies in industries such as online services, investment planning and brokerage, and senior-assisted living are inaugurating such strategies to enhance employment practices, generate better job fit, and ensure that they're able to provide high-quality, knowledge-intensive services to customers. They are also doing it to enhance employee retention and assure preservation of their organizational cultures, viewing such steps as key to retaining their marketplace position. We foresee this trend becoming even more widespread, as demand for scarce, highly educated knowledge workers grows, and as more and more companies become intentional about long-term knowledge management and development of intellectual capital.

Web-based learning will become the standard training and employee development channel in companies because it is an ideal way to drive change and leverage knowledge enterprise-wide. The future of technology-based training appears to have unlimited potential. It can be used to facilitate course customization, integrate just-in-time learning with daily work tasks, and deliver formerly classroom-based training to multiple sites simultaneously—often for a fraction of the cost. Even more important, Web-based learning offers companies the opportunity to create online professional communities and working groups for problem-solving purposes, strategic planning, product R&D, and other tasks, something many futurists view as the foundation for tomorrow's increasingly decentralized and "virtual" organizations. Because of its ability to integrate functions and facilitate communication, the growth of Web-based learning will become a key transformation tool for organizations in the coming century, as companies find it necessary to revise best practices on a more frequent basis, incorporate new learning into business operations, and bring greater speed and quality to their R&D efforts.

While the preceding issues will offer companies strategic, tactical, logistical, and organizational challenges, executives must consider still other issues as companies go increasingly global and become "global business citizens" in an increasingly interdependent world.

First, to survive and thrive in the next century, companies and executives must develop a truly global perspective about the nature of business and markets. In the world of tomorrow, it will be critical that businesspeople possess (if they don't already) the ability to see the world economy as a vast "ecosystem" of economic, technological, and political forces, all shaping and reshaping the business environment on a continuous basis. In this world, national boundaries will cease to be critical determinants of markets or business dominance, and the advent of electronic commerce will offer the promise of greater community and human understanding in addition to greater market access.

At the same time, the need will exist for companies to move swiftly and deftly in some cases, not just to take advantage of the marketplace opportunities but also to forestall public relations problems that may stem from concerns about product reliability or consumer safety. One soft-drink manufacturer discovered this in June 1999 when concerns quickly arose in Europe about the safety of its products and almost immediately affected the company's share price on Wall Street. This reaction as one newspaper commentator put it at the time, represents "the flip side of globalization." A growing number of multinationals have discovered that in today's global marketplace, it isn't just capital and technology that flow across national borders, but also rumors and new coverage.

Suffice it to say that in today's global marketplace no multinational corporation can afford consumer missteps or PR snafus, since the sun is always shining on some market for its products.

The executives (and companies) that succeed in the twenty-first century business environment will be *visionary, culturally inclusive, environmentally sensitive,* and *attuned to balancing the need for ethics with profits.* We are not here to philosophize about the humanitarian, environmental, or social ramifications of business change. Yet in a global, digital, and electronically interconnected world, such issues cannot be separated from those of business. Witness what a company like Royal Dutch Shell is doing today to pursue both "profits and principles" in its business dealings throughout the world. The impetus for doing this came as Shell, in reinventing itself, recognized how out of touch it had been in much of the world in which it operated just a few years ago. Because of this realization, it integrated a statement of ethical principles into its business charter.

Second, as we move toward a global economy, companies and nations must avoid creating a technological/digital divide that separates the information "haves" from the information "have nots," thus creating a world of the affluent and the economically dispossessed. Alarm bells are already being sounded that the potential for this problem to occur exists.

In the United States, "there is a growing digital divide," according to Philip Burgess, President of the Center for the New West, an advocacy group whose board includes Solomon Trujillo, CEO of regional phone giant US West, and Utah Governor Michael Leavitt. The gulf, Burgess warns, could have significant implications for the social and economic fabric of many communities, particularly those in less densely populated parts of the United States.[4]

The problem of an emerging digital divide becomes more pronounced when one looks outside the United States. At the 1998 World Congress on Information Technology in Fairfax, Virginia, economist Jeffrey Sachs, Director of the Harvard Institute for International Development, sounded a warning about the volatility that may become an endemic part of world globalization efforts unless companies, industries, and nations work to avoid a world of information "haves" and "have nots."[5]

"As a macroeconomist, I believe the greatest challenge that world society faces [today] is the challenge of economic development for the still five-sixths of the world's planet that find themselves in material conditions far behind those of the advanced countries," noted Sachs.[5] Sounding a note of caution to those in business and society that view all forms of globalization, electronic connectivity, and economic expansion in emerging markets as good things, he observed, "changes in information technology will redraw the map" of who has economic power and who does not. For while Western countries and their economies have benefited greatly from the IT revolution as has much of Asia, virtually all of Africa has been excluded from the process, he noted.[5]

For the reasons we've just outlined, therefore, we should not assume that advances in technology (like instantaneous communications and Internet accessibility) will automatically be a rising tide that lifts all boats for all people.

Finally, in the twenty-first century, companies will need to get away from the "next quarter" mindset in managing their bottom-lines. We noted at the beginning of this book the importance of companies doing scenario planning in order to imagine their futures. Yet again, there is still a relatively strong bias against this approach, at least in American business. Many American businesspeople and Wall Streeters are, by nature, short-term oriented in their thinking. The next quarter, in their minds, is all that counts. That, of course, militates against a more disciplined approach and discerning understanding of developments in today's business climate with long-term implications for us all. Ironically, the current prosperity within the American economy may, in some ways, actually militate against businesspeople taking the kind of long-range global view of business and economic interdependence that will be essential to individual, business, community, and national prosperity in the *next* century.

Chapter Conclusions

Despite the challenges and concerns we've just enumerated, we're hopeful about the future, otherwise we wouldn't have written this book. Moreover, we've seen many organizations overcome organizational entropy, factionalism, political divisiveness, and other shortcomings to create climates in which real and sustainable organizational renewal can be both born and sustained. You've seen a cross section of them in these pages.

We live in exciting times. The global economy is becoming a reality, and the future will be filled not only with new business opportunities for companies—born of the business climate shifts we've outlined in this book—but also with exciting new jobs and careers, spawned in industries such as pharmaceuticals, financial services, health care, and computers. The future is bright, for both individuals and organizations. What's needed is for business leaders to possess the tactical and strategic leadership skills not just to effect change, but also to develop people, build strategic partnerships and alliances, and remain "environmentally vigilant" to changes in the business climate with implications for their organizations.

It has been our goal in this book to let you listen in to conversations we've had with some of today's most successful "change makers" in business. By letting these individuals tell you their transformation stories *in their own words*, we believe we've provided you with a powerful set of ideas, learnings, principles, and practices that you can use to be an effective change maker yourself. As we've said, there is no single "shake-and-bake" recipe for managing change. Every organization's experience of it will be a little different. Still, you can take steps to optimize success with transformation efforts and to achieve measurable and concrete results in the process. We hope this book proves to be a valuable companion and road guide to you in that endeavor.

For more information about *Business Climate Shifts: Profiles of Change Makers*, please visit the PricewaterhouseCoopers website (PricewaterhouseCoopers.com) and enter the search words, "Business Climate Shifts."

W. Warner Burke
William Trahant
Richard Koonce

NOTES

Chapter 1

1. Dr. Neal Lane, Director of the National Science Foundation, in remarks delivered to the World Congress on Information Technology, George Mason University, Fairfax, Virginia, June 23, 1998.

2. Dr. Howard Frank, Dean of the College of Business and Management at the University of Maryland at College Park, in remarks delivered to the World Congress on Information Technology, George Mason University, Fairfax, Virginia, June 24, 1998.

3. William Greider, *One World, Ready or Not: The Manic Logic of Global Capitalism* (New York: Simon & Schuster, 1997), p. 15.

4. Don Tapscott, *The Digital Economy: Promise and Peril in the Age of Networked Intelligence* (New York: McGraw-Hill, 1996), p. 10.

5. Matthew Kiernan, *The Eleven Commandments of 21st Century Management* (Englewood Cliffs: Prentice-Hall, 1996), p. 7.

6. Stephen Rhinesmith, *A Manager's Guide to Globalization* (Chicago: Irwin Professional Publishing, 1996), p. 26.

7. Matthew Kiernan, *The Eleven Commandments of 21st Century Management* (Englewood Cliffs: Prentice-Hall, 1996), p. 2.

8. Peter Schwartz, *The Art of the Long View* (New York: Doubleday, 1996), p. 38.

9. Carey Goldberg and Gina Kolata, "Scientists Announce Birth of Cows Cloned in New Way," *The New York Times*, January 21, 1998.

10. Justin Gillis, "Cows and Clones on a Va. Pharm," *The Washington Post*, Sunday, Feb. 28, 1999.

11. John Welch, Jr., "A Matter of Exchange Rates," *Wall Street Journal*, June 21, 1994.

12. Steve Yearout, "The Secrets of Improvement-Driven Organizations," *Quality Progress*, January 1996.

Chapter 2

1. Typically, the questions asked in organizational assessments are highly tailored to the needs of an organization. Moreover, question sets are far more detailed than this brief sample suggests.

2. Besides gathering information from respondents in each of these areas, assessments also collect demographic data that enable a company to categorize findings by age, function, departmental area, or other criteria. This way, one can localize data if and when appropriate. For example, when change efforts relate to specific organizational units or departments.

Chapter 4

1. "How to Make Mergers Work," *The Economist*, January 9–15, 1999.

2. Robert Bauman, Peter Jackson, and Joanne Lawrence, *From Promise to Performance: A Journey of Transformation at SmithKline Beecham* (Boston: Harvard Business School Press, 1997), p. 255.

3. Ibid.

Chapter 10

1. You'll recall that technology is a *transactional* variable in the performance of organizations; strategy, a *transformational* variable. The latter is a much stronger driver of change than the former. The exception to this rule is when we consider technology in broad terms; that is, when a scientific discovery or technical breakthrough (e.g., the microchip) occurs that affects an entire industry. In such instances, technology becomes a force within the organization's external environment and, therefore, a transformational change factor.

2. These findings are drawn from a Coopers & Lybrand study titled "Customer Care as a Competitive Response: Leveraging Information

Across the Enterprise," conducted by Bill Rossello and Jerry Sequiera in 1996. The findings were subsequently published in an article, "The Care and Feeding of Customers," by Wayne Wilhelm and Bill Rossello, which appeared in the March 1997 edition of *Management Review*. The case studies shared in this chapter (USAA, Mercedes-Benz, and Sun MicroSystems) are adapted with permission from that article.

Epilogue

1. Barnaby Feder, "Getting Biotechnology Set to Hatch," *The New York Times*, May 2, 1998.

2. Bob Tedeschi, E-Commerce Report, "Affiliate Referrals Generate Big Profits," *The New York Times*, March 22, 1999.

3. Robert Reich, *The Work of Nations* (New York: Vintage Books, 1992), p. 83.

4. Chris O'Malley, et al, "The Digital Divide," *Time*, March 22, 1999.

5. Dr. Jeffrey Sachs, Director of the Harvard University Institute for International Development, in remarks delivered to the World Congress on Information Technology, George Mason University, Fairfax, Virginia, June 22, 1998.

REFERENCES AND SUGGESTED READING

Bauman, Robert, Peter Jackson, and Joanne Lawrence. *From Promise to Performance: A Journey of Transformation at SmithKline Beecham*. Boston: Harvard Business School Press, 1997.

Browning John. *Pocket Information Technology*. London: The Economist Newspaper Ltd., 1997.

Burke, W. Warner. *Organization Development: A Process of Learning and Changing*. New York: Addison-Wesley, 1992.

Burroughs, William, et al. *The Nature Company Guides: Weather*. San Francisco: Time-Life Books and The Nature Company, 1996.

Dowson, John, Wood T. Parker, et al. *Postal Performance: The Transformation of a Global Industry*. Mansfield, Ohio: Bookmasters, Inc., 1997.

Dauphinais, G. William, and Colin Price. *Straight from the CEO*. New York: Simon & Schuster, 1998.

"How to Make Mergers Work," *The Economist.*, January 9, 1999.

Feder, Barnaby. "Getting Biotechnology Set to Hatch," *The New York Times*, May 2, 1998.

Gates, Bill. *Business@ The Speed of Thought*. New York: Warner Books, 1999.

Gillis, Justin. "Cows and Clones on a Virginia Pharm," *The Washington Post*, February 28, 1999.

Goldberg, Carey, and Gina Kolata. "Scientists Announce Births of Cows Cloned in New Way," *New York Times*, January 21, 1998.

Greider, William. *One World, Ready or Not: The Manic Logic of Global Capitalism*. New York: Simon & Schuster, 1997.

Grove, Andrew. *Only the Paranoid Survive*. New York: Doubleday, 1996. *Harvard Business Review on Change*. Boston: Harvard Business School Press, 1998.

Hamel, Gary, and C.K. Prahalad. *Competing for the Future*. Boston: Harvard Business School Press, 1994.

Jones, Tim. *Euro Essentials*. London: The Economist Newspaper Ltd, 1998.

Kiernan, Matthew. *The 11 Commandments of 21st Century Management*. Englewood Cliffs, NJ: Prentice-Hall, 1996.

Kotter, John. *The New Rules: Eight Business Breakthroughs to Career Success in the 21st Century*. New York: Free Press, 1995.

Naisbitt, John. *Megatrends Asia*. New York: Touchstone, 1997.

O'Malley, Chris, et al. "The Digital Divide," *Time*, March 22, 1999.

Reich, Robert. *The Work of Nations*. New York: Vintage Books, 1992.

Rhinesmith, Stephen. *A Manager's Guide to Globalization*. Chicago: Irwin Publishing, 1996.

Ross, Gerald, and Michael Kay. *Toppling the Pyramids: Redefining the Way Companies Run*. New York: Random House, 1994.

Schwartz, Peter. *The Art of the Long View*. New York: Doubleday, 1996.

Sun Tzu. *The Art of War*. Boston: Shambhala Publications, Inc., 1991.

Tapscott, Don. *The Digital Economy*. New York: McGraw-Hill, 1996.

Tapscott, Don, and Art Caston. *Paradigm Shift: The New Promise of Information Technology*. New York: McGraw-Hill, 1993.

Tedeschi, Bob. E-Commerce Report: "Affiliate Referrals Generate Big Profits," The *New York Times*, March 22, 1999.

Tichy, Noel. *The Leadership Engine*. New York: HarperBusiness, 1997.

Welch, John F. "A Matter of Exchange Rates," *Wall Street Journal*, June 21, 1994.

Wilhelm, Wayne, and William Rossello. "The Care and Feeding of Customers," *Management Review*, March 1997.

Yearout, Steve. "The Secrets of Improvement-Driven Organizations," *Quality Progress,* January, 1996.

INDEX

WARNER BURKE, Ph.D.

W. Warner Burke is Professor of Psychology and Education, and Chair of the Department of Organization and Leadership at Teachers College, Columbia University.

The author or editor of 13 books on business change, including **ORGANIZATION DEVELOPMENT:** *A Process of Learning and Changing* (Addison Wesley, 1994) he is one of the leading thinkers and consultants in the field of change management in corporate America today.

Dr. Burke's client list reads like a Who's Who of American and International Business. He worked closely with Lord Colin Marshall, Chairman of British Airways and Dr. Nick Georgiades, Head of HR to help turn that airline into one of the world's most popular and profitable air carriers. He also played a pivotal role in helping to bring about the merger of U.S.-based Smith-Kline Beckman and British-based Beecham to form SmithKline Beecham, one of the world's largest and most successful integrated healthcare companies. Dr. Burke's work on behalf of SB is discussed in depth in the book, **From Promise to Performance:** *A Journey of Transformation at SmithKline Beecham* by Robert Bauman, Peter Jackson and Joanne Lawrence, published by Harvard Business School Press. Other current and former clients of Dr. Burke's include NASA, British Aerospace, The British Broadcasting Company, The Dime Savings Bank of New York, Alliance Capital, Mt. Sinai Hospital, and Equitable.

Dr. Burke is a Fellow of The Academy of Management, the American Psychological Society, and The Society of Industrial and Organizational Psychology. He is also a Diplomate in Industrial/Organizational Psychology, American Board of Professional Psychology. He is past editor of the American Management Association's quarterly publication, *Organizational Dynamics,* and founded and served as initial editor for The *Academy of Management Executive.*

Dr. Burke is the recipient of numerous awards, including The NASA Public Service Medal, The "Distinguished Contribution to Human Resource Development" Award, presented by The American Society for Training & Development, and the "Organization Development Professional Practice Area Award for Excellence", also awarded by ASTD.

A former member of the Board of Governors of The Academy of Management and The American Society for Training & Development, Dr. Burke designed and served as faculty director of the Columbia Business School's executive program, "Leading and Managing People" from 1988 to 1995.

WILLIAM TRAHANT

Bill Trahant is a Senior Partner with Price-waterhouseCoopers Consulting in Fairfax, Virginia. He has more than 20 years of diverse consulting experience in the public and commercial sectors, and is the PwC Partner responsible for overseeing the firm's Organization and Change Strategy engagements throughout North and South America. In this capacity, he leads the development and execution of the Firm's consulting methodologies, thought leadership activities, and strategic business alliances. He is also responsible for quality oversight on Organization and Change Strategy engagements directly under his purview, and in collaboration with other parts of PricewaterhouseCoopers Consulting.

Over the course of his career, Bill has provided a broad spectrum of advisory services to public and private sector clients including government departments and agencies, manufacturing companies, consumer goods organizations, financial institutions and medical device companies. Specific clients include Royal Dutch Shell, GE Capital, Air Products, American Electric Power, The United States Postal Service, Pennsylvania Power & Light, AlliedSignal Corporation, NationsBank, Premier Bank, Owens-Illinois, Prudential Insurance, ConvaTec and CODELCO.

Mr. Trahant is co-author (with David Carr and Kelvin Hard) **of MANAGING THE CHANGE PROCESS: *A Field Book for Change Agents, Consultants, Team Leaders and Reengineering Managers*** (McGraw-Hill, 1995). He has also written on the topics of leadership, productivity, process redesign, and organizational change for numerous business publications, *including Management Review, Executive Excellence, Training & Development, Bank Marketing, Government Executive, National Productivity Review* and others.

A member of the Council of Governors of The American Society for Training & Development, Mr. Trahant is a much-sought after speaker on the topic of organizational transformation. He speaks frequently on leadership and quality topics at business conferences and industry gatherings, including those organized by The Conference Board. He has also been interviewed by the business press on the topics of leadership, organizational change and corporate transformation.

RICHARD KOONCE

Collaborator

Richard Koonce is an accomplished interviewer, radio commentator, author, and business consultant who has had occasion to interview scores of business leaders, public figures, and well-known personalities over the years ranging from Robert Reich and Dan Rather to Deborah Tannen, Jesse Helms, Bob Dole, Howard K. Smith, Gerald Ford, James Michener and Timothy Leary, among others.

A former broadcast journalist and contributing commentator to Public Radio's "Marketplace" Program (heard on over 200 public radio stations in the United States) Richard is known for his ability to extract lively, incisive, and revealing interviews from people in all walks of life, having conducted hundreds of interviews for various writing and interview projects in the course of a 20-year journalistic and business career.

Besides his work as an interviewer, Richard is also a consultant to PricewaterhouseCoopers Consulting and a nationally known expert on job and workplace trends. The author of *CAREER POWER! 12 Winning Habits to Get You From Where You Are to Where You Are to Where You Want To Be* (Amacom, 1994), he has been interviewed by *The New York Times, The Wall Street Journal, Money Magazine, U.S. News and World Report, USA Today, The Washington Post, Glamour, Good Housekeeping* and *Working Woman*, among others.

Butterworth–Heinemann Business Books . . . for Transforming Business

Life Work Transitions.Com: Putting Your Spirit Online
Deborah L. Knox and Sandra S. Butzel, 0-7506-7160-2

A Little Knowledge Is A Dangerous Thing: Understanding Our Global Knowledge Economy
Dale Neef, 0-7506-7061-4

Marketing Plans that Work: Targeting Growth and Profitability
Malcolm H.B. McDonald and Warren J. Keegan, 0-7506-9828-4

Navigating Cross-Cultural Ethics: What Global Managers Do Right to Keep From Going Wrong
Eileen Morgan, 0-7506-9915-9

A Place to Shine: Emerging from the Shadows at Work
Daniel S. Hanson, 0-7506-9738-5

Power Partnering: A Strategy for Business Excellence in the 21st Century
Sean Gadman, 0-7506-9809-8

Putting Emotional Intelligence to Work; Successful Leadership Is More Than IQ
David Ryback, 0-7506-9956-6

Quantum Leaps: 7 Skills for Workplace ReCreation
Charlotte A. Shelton, 0-7506-7077-0

Resources for the Knowledge-Based Economy Series Knowledge Management and Organizational Design
Paul S. Myers, 0-7506-9749-0

Knowledge Management Tools
Rudy L. Ruggles, III, 0-7506-9849-7

Knowledge in Organizations
Laurence Prusak, 0-7506-9718-0

The Strategic Management of Intellectual Capital
David A. Klein, 0-7506-9850-0

Rise of the Knowledge Worker
James W. Cortada, 0-7506-7058-4

The Knowledge Economy
Dale Neef, 0-7506-9936-1

The Economic Impact of Knowledge
Dale Neef, G. Anthony Seisfeld, and Jacquelyn Cefola, 0-7506-7009-6

Knowledge and Special Libraries
James A. Matarazzo and Suzanne D. Connolly, 0-7506-7084-3

Knowledge and Strategy
Michael Zack, 0-7506-7088-6

To purchase a copy of any Butterworth–Heinemann Business title, please visit your local bookstore or call 1-800-366-2665.